OTHER PEOPLE'S MONEY:

The Ultimate Seduction

◆

Jerry Sterner

THEATRE BOOK PUBLISHERS

An Applause Original
OTHER PEOPLE'S MONEY
Copyright © 1989 by Jerry Sterner
All Rights Reserved.

All inquiries concerning publication rights including book club, translation and anthology rights should be addressed to Applause Theatre Book Publishers, 211 W. 71st St., New York, NY 10023.

All inquiries concerning stock and amateur performing rights should be directed to Samuel French, Inc., 45 West 25th St., New York, NY 10010.

Inquiries concerning all other rights should be addressed to William Morris Agency, Inc., 1350 Avenue of the Americas, New York, NY 10019, Attn: Esther Sherman.

Library of Congress Cataloging-in-publication data:

Sterner, Jerry.
   Other people's money / by Jerry Sterner.
      p.   cm.
   ISBN 1-55783-062-2 : $14.95. — ISBN 1-55783-061-4 (pbk.) : $7.95
   I. Title.
PS3569.T432508   1990
812'.54—dc20   90-30151
                                                                        CIP

APPLAUSE THEATRE BOOK PUBLISHERS
211 W. 71st Street
New York, NY 10023
212/595-4735

First Applause Printing, 1990

Quality printing and binding by:
Haddon Craftsmen
1001 Wyoming Ave.
Scranton, PA 18509

OTHER PEOPLE'S MONEY

◆

"OTHER PEOPLE'S MONEY" was originally presented by
The American Stage Company, Teaneck, New Jersey.
The Play was subsequently presented by **Hartford Stage Company**.

The Hartford Stage Company production of the Play was presented
Off Broadway by **Jeffrey Ash** and **Susan Quint Gallin** in association
with **Dennis Grimaldi** at the Minetta Lane Theatre in New York
City. The Play opened February 16, 1989 with the following cast:

William Coles	**James Murtaugh**
Andrew Jorgenson	**Arch Johnson**
Bea Sullivan	**Scotty Bloch**
Lawrence Garfinkle	**Kevin Conway**
Kate Sullivan	**Mercedes Ruehl**

CAST

William Coles Mid-forties. Attractive, polished, President of New England Wire and Cable.

Andrew Jorgenson Chairman of New England Wire and Cable, 68 years of age.

Bea Sullivan Longtime assistant and friend of Jorgenson. An attractive woman in her early sixties.

Lawrence Garfinkle An obese, elegant, cunning New York "takeover artist." About forty.

Kate Sullivan Bea's daughter. An attractive, sexy, Wall Street attorney, about thirty-five.

SETTING
New York and Rhode Island.

TIME
The present.

ACT ONE

Stage is dark. After a short pause, Bill Coles, *an attractive, well-groomed man in his mid-forties, emerges from the darkness and walks Downstage Center where a spotlight awaits him. He pauses a beat.*

Coles: It's been said that you have to be a storyteller to tell a story. It's also been said that businessmen aren't good storytellers . . . not that we don't have a story to tell . . . we do. We tell it in numbers: you know, sales, earnings, dividends. We also express it in ratios: net worth to long term debt, long term debt to working capital. And we tell it every year. Have you ever read an Annual Report? . . . We're not good storytellers.

Which is too bad. For there's an important story that needs to be told. It goes way beyond numbers. It's about loyalty, tradition, friendship and of course, money. Lots of money. It's one heck of a story. And if it hasn't already affected your life, it will. *(Smiles.)* It affected mine. It only started a few years back. We were all naive, then. But you know something? I knew. I knew as soon as the Old Man told me about our expected visitor.

Lights up on Andrew Jorgenson's *office. Throughout the play scene shifts occur with some rapidity. Rather than formal sets, locations are suggested by playing area, lights, platforms, etc., as the director, set designer and budget allow.* Jorgenson *sits behind a modest desk in his office. He's sixty-eight, a good looking man in good physical condition. He's a "hands on" type, more comfortable with his sleeves rolled up tinkering with a machine than sitting in a boardroom. He speaks to an unseen* Coles.

Jorgenson: Why are you so nervous? Stop acting like

an expectant father.

Coles: *(Entering from Center Stage.)* I heard that name before.

Jorgenson: So what?

Coles: Why would he come all the way from New York? We've never had anyone from New York before.

Jorgenson: Sure we have. Had someone directly from Wall Street a couple of years back.

Coles: I've been here twelve years. I've never seen anyone south of Connecticut.

Jorgenson: . . . Twelve years? Has it been that long? . . . The guy was sitting right there—all stiff and proper, taking notes on a clipboard. Some kind of analyst. Wouldn't get close to any of the walls. Scared of a little dust. Three piece suit, pointy shoes, tie up to here. He starts asking me all kinds of questions and I noticed he wasn't looking at me, looking at the wall back there. I turn around and wouldn't you know—meanest looking spider was halfway up the ceiling. You know what he says? Bill, you listening? He says, "Could you please get someone to dispose of it?" Not kill it, mind you—dispose of it. I told him since he was the one with the pointy shoes the job was his. *(Laughs at the memory.)* Didn't ask another question. Got up and left. Didn't even say goodbye.

Coles: Be careful what you say to him.

Jorgenson: Don't worry about me. Better check for spiders. *(Rises, put's an arm around* Coles' *shoulder.)* C'mon. C'mon. I was joking. I've never seen you this way.

Coles: Let me do the talking.

Jorgenson: You do the talking. I'll do the listening. "Nu Yawkas" are fun to listen to . . . Where the hell was that guy from? . . . Aha—Barney Smith.

Coles: Smith, Barney.

Jorgenson: Smith, Barney. Figures. Wall Street generally does things ass-backwards.

Coles: Have you looked at our stock lately?

Jorgenson: I already got a call from Ossie at the bank. Happier than a pig in shit. Told me it's up a couple of points. He owns fifteen thousand shares, you know. Has for years. I remember the day he bought. Same day I was made President. I was really scared. He called. Told me he was buying stock to show his confidence in me. Told me he wouldn't sell till I retired. The man kept his word for . . . thirty-eight years now.

Coles: More shares traded in the last month than did all of last year.

Jorgenson: Bill, what's wrong with you? The stock is going up. Worry when the stock goes down.

Bea *enters hurriedly. She's excited.*

Bea: Come. Look. Look! *(She ushers them to the window.)* Is that something, Jorgy?

Jorgenson: That's a goddamned big car.

Coles: It's a stretch limo.

Bea: *(To* Jorgenson.*)* You see—manners. The chauffeur gets out first, walks all the way around . . . opens the
door. You could learn from that, Jorgy.

Jorgenson: Goddamned big car.

Lights up on Garfinkle, *cross stage. He is an immense man of
forty, though he looks older. He is always elegantly dressed,
surprisingly graceful for his bulk. He is, in some way, larger
than life. His deep, rich voice fills the stage. He looks about.*

Garfinkle: Haven't seen a place this shitty since I left
the Bronx.

Bea: *(Moving to* Garfinkle, *her hand extended.)* Welcome.
You must be Lawrence Garfinkle. I'm Bea Sullivan. Mr.
Jorgenson's assistant. He's expecting you. *(She shakes his
hand. They begin walking to* Jorgenson's *office.)* Would you
like to invite your chauffeur in? We have a small reception
area he could wait in—keep warm.

Garfinkle: He's a "yard" chauffeur. Bring him inside
and you'll spoil him.

Bea: . . . Right this way, please. *(They enter office.)* This
is Mr. Jorgenson, our Chairman. Mr. Coles, our President. Mr. Garfinkle.

Jorgenson: Call me Jorgy. Everybody else does. *(Moves
from his desk. They shake.)* Welcome to New England Wire
and Cable.

Coles: How do you do, Mr. Garfinkle?

Garfinkle: I do good. Mind if I have a seat? I do even
better when I sit.

Jorgenson: *(Laughs.)* I know what you mean.

Garfinkle *dusts off chair with a handkerchief.*

Uh-oh, Bill ... better check for spiders. *(Moving to Garfinkle.)* Wire and Cable is man's work. Gotta expect a little grime.

Bea: May I get you some coffee?

Garfinkle: Is there a Dunkin' Donuts in this town?

Bea: Dunkin' Donuts? ...

Jorgenson: Never saw one.

Garfinkle: Crispy Cremes? ... Something?

Jorgenson: There's Sam's on Beaver. Doesn't he make donuts?

Bea: I believe he does. He'd be your best bet. Just make a left when you leave the plant. Beaver is your second—

Garfinkle: *(Taking a large roll of cash from his pocket and handing* Bea *several bills.)* Why don't you be a sweetheart and take a ride with Arthur and pick up a couple of dozen. Bring one here and leave one in the car for the trip back.

Bea: ... They might not have much of a selection. Which kind do you like?

Garfinkle: I like them all. *(Smiling for the first time.)* Can't you tell?

Bea *exits.*

Jorgenson: Have a nice ride, Bea. You watch, she's going to take him the long way to Beaver. What'd you say your first name was?

Garfinkle: Lawrence.

Jorgenson: Larry, you made her day. Last limo we saw up here was in '48 when Harry Truman was running for President. Came right here to the plant. *(Takes him to window.)* Stood right out there. Right there. Gave a speech. Just after the war. It was the golden age, rebuilding America and all. Had thirty-five hundred men working right here. Right at this plant. Going twenty-four hours a day, seven days a week. Truman gave a fine talk. Very impressive. Only Democrat I ever voted for.

Coles: What can we do for you, Mr. Garfinkle? What brings a busy man like you up this way?

Garfinkle: Harry Truman stories don't grab you, huh?

Coles: We're all busy.

Garfinkle: You're right. Let's do business. I got a computer back in New York. Call her Carmen. Every morning when I wake up—before I even brush my teeth, I punch out, "Carmen, computer on the wall, who's the fairest of them all?" You'll forgive me—my programmer isn't Shakespeare.

Coles: Go on.

Garfinkle: Most mornings she spits out, "You are, Garfinkle, you're the fairest of them all." But once in a while, maybe two, three times a year she says something else. Six weeks ago she said: "Garfinkle, Garfinkle, scratch your balls, New England Wire and Cable is the fairest of them all." *(Jorgenson laughs.)* I thought it was funny, too. And I do it again. "Carmen computer on the wall, who's the fairest of them all?" She responds, "Don't be a schmuck, Garfinkle—do the numbers!"

Coles: I'm interested. Do the numbers.

Garfinkle: Get a paper and pencil. Carmen will educate you.

Coles *takes a pad and pencil from* Jorgenson's *desk.*

The Wire and Cable business is a little soft. Has been for the last ten years. What's it worth?

Jorgenson: This would not be a good time to—

Garfinkle: I know. I'm not blaming you. You've done a hell of a job. You've kept it alive. That's an accomplishment. Carmen agrees. I'll bet she thinks it's worth more than you do. She says you got equipment up here that cost 120 million. Worth, even at salvage, 30 to 35 million. Write down 30 million. How many acres you got here?

Coles: One hundred ten.

Garfinkle: What's that worth?

Jorgenson: It would depend on what it's used for.

Garfinkle: Worst case basis. Grazing land. Ten million fair? *(Coles nods.)* Good. Write down ten million. Put it underneath the thirty.

Jorgenson: We have other businesses, you know. Bill

here has diversified us a good deal. He's done a hell of a job, despite my kicking and screaming.

Coles: What does Carmen think the rest of the company is worth, Mr. Garfinkle?

Garfinkle: Let's see ... what do you got? Plumbing supplies, electrical distribution, adhesives ... boring. Nothing my friends on the street would get excited about. But dependable. Decent cash flow.

Jorgenson: With our cumulative losses at Wire and Cable we keep all the earnings from our other businesses. We haven't paid federal taxes in years.

Garfinkle: You haven't made money in years.

Jorgenson: It'll turn. We got a good crew up here. Best in the business. When it does, we're gonna knock their socks off.

Garfinkle: Everything is possible. Maybe a Dunkin' Donuts will open up next door.

Coles: What does your computer tell you the rest of our businesses are worth, Mr. Garfinkle?

Garfinkle: Conservative ... six times cash flow.

Coles: We had ten million in flow last year. This year we're projecting a fifteen per cent increase.

Garfinkle: Carmen only knows what happened. She can't predict. Write down sixty ... underneath the ten.

Coles: What else, Mr. Garfinkle?

Garfinkle: Working capital. You got twenty-five million—ten million of it in cash—write down twenty-five.

Coles: Anything else?

Garfinkle: Add it up. What do you got?

Coles: One hundred and twenty-five million.

Garfinkle: Good. Now let's say Carmen was suffering from pre-menstrual syndrome. (*Jorgenson looks at him quizzically.*) A little crazed. Too optimistic. Forget twenty-five million. Take it off. What do you got?

Coles: One hundred million.

Garfinkle: Nice round number. I like nice round numbers. Now make a line. Right down the middle of the page. Start a new column. Call it liabilities. Let's see what you got. Any debt?

Jorgenson: Not a penny. Don't believe in it.

Garfinkle: Any lawsuits? Any environmental bullshit?

Jorgenson: None. We've complied with every law. That's a good part of our losses right there.

Garfinkle: Pension liabilities?

Coles: Fully funded.

Garfinkle: Ok. Add it up. What do you got?

Jorgenson: Didn't write anything.

Garfinkle: That's exactly what I said to Carmen. Now here comes the fun part. How many shares you got outstanding?

Coles: Four million.

Garfinkle: Divide four million into the hundred million. What do you got?

Coles: Twenty-five.

Garfinkle: Good. Now that was all foreplay. Let's go for the real thing. What's your stock selling at?

Coles: You know very well what it's selling at, Mr. Garfinkle.

Garfinkle: Aw, don't do that. I came all the way from New York. Don't break my rhythm. Let me do my thing. What's the stock at?

Coles: Ten—before you started buying.

Garfinkle: That's ten for a twenty-five dollar number. Forty cents on the dollar. Carmen almost came. I had to change my underwear.

Jorgenson: This is a fine company, Larry. We've worked hard. We have a nice little story to tell but unless you make those little micro-chips or fry chicken it's hard to interest you money guys on Wall Street.

Coles: How many shares have you bought?

Garfinkle: One hundred and ninety-six thousand. I recognize a good job when I see it. I'm happy to put my money here.

Jorgenson: *(Laughing.)* I'll have to tell Ossie at the bank. He'll be mighty grateful to you. If you have time we'll have lunch together. Get him to spring for it. Tell him you're selling if he don't spring for it. Ossie's tighter than a duck's ass. How'd you figure out to buy such an odd amount? Why not two hundred thousand—nice even number. I thought you liked even numbers.

Coles: Two hundred thousand is five percent of our shares. At five percent he has to file a 13-D with the Securities and Exchange Commission. It then becomes public knowledge. *(To* Garfinkle.*)* Plan on buying more?

Garfinkle: Never can tell. Got to talk to Carmen.

Jorgenson: That's his business, Bill. He'll let us know when he wants to . . . or when he has to. It's nice to know you have that confidence in us. Nice to have you as a stockholder.

Garfinkle: Don't let me down. Get us to twenty-five. That's what we're worth.

Jorgenson: You know I can't control that. We do the best we can running the company. I can promise you one thing—we spend the stockholder's money with care. We don't squander it.

Garfinkle: Not on paint at any rate.

Jorgenson: Not on anything. You watch the nickels and dimes and the dollars take care of themselves. My dad always said that. He founded this company. I guess I do too. As true today as when he said it.

Bea *enters with a bag of donuts.*

Bea, Larry here is our newest stockholder. Give the man a donut.

Bea: All they had was honey and whole wheat. I left six of each in the car.

She holds out the bag. Garfinkle *takes one out, grimaces, and puts it back.*

Jorgenson: How was the ride?

Bea: Everyone stared. It's got a television, a bar, telephone, stock quote machine—

Jorgenson: And now donuts. If you have no objection, Larry, we're going to call you the "donut man."

Garfinkle: Where's my change?

Bea: *(Handing him the change.)* Oh—I'm sorry. Just a little flustered, I guess . . . sorry.

Garfinkle: I like to watch the nickels and dimes, too. (Garfinkle *takes the bag and exits the playing area. They stare after him for a beat.)*

Jorgenson: So you really like being chauffeured around? I thought you'd be embarrassed.

Bea: Jorgy, riding in a limousine is not an aquired taste. One takes to it all at once.

Lights out in Jorgenson's *office. Lights up Center Stage.* Garfinkle *is alone checking out the donuts.*

Garfinkle: Whole wheat and honey?! What—do I look sick? You eat this when you're sick—with tea. Step on it, Arthur. This whole goddamned place stinks. Make sure you get the car washed when we get home. *(Garfinkle exits.)*

Coles *moves to Center Stage. Lights up on* Garfinkle's *office as* Coles *enters.*

Coles: That's an impressive office you have out there.

Garfinkle: No big deal. Only lawyers. What can I do for you?

Coles: Thanks for seeing me on such short notice. I'm not really here on business. My wife and I came down to spend the evening with Bill, Jr. He's attending Columbia. Got two more after him. Both girls. Claire's out shopping now. It's always a treat to come to this city.

Garfinkle: Great.

Coles: We're from small towns in Florida. Met at Florida State—

Garfinkle: What'd you come here for—to give me your biography?

Coles: I didn't know I was boring you.

Garfinkle: Now you know.

Coles: *(Trying to control himself.)* . . . I'll get to the point. I see by the latest 13-D you hold just over four hundred thousand shares. That's ten per cent.

Garfinkle: Four hundred and twenty-five thousand. Bought some this morning.

Coles: The filing said they were purchased for "investment purposes only."

Garfinkle: I never read filings.

Coles: What does "investment purposes only" mean?

Garfinkle: Means I bought them to make money.

Coles: How much more do you intend on buying?

Garfinkle: That's none of your business.

Coles: Can we speak frankly?

Garfinkle: No. Lie to me. Tell me how thrilled you are to know me. Tell me how gorgeous I am.

Coles: You don't want to speak frankly?

Garfinkle: I always speak frankly. I don't like people who say "Can we speak frankly?" Means they're bullshitting me the rest of the time.

Coles: I'm sorry. I won't use that phrase any more.

Garfinkle: What do you want?

Coles: Two years. I want two years.

Garfinkle: For what?

Coles: Jorgenson is sixty-eight. In two years he'll be

seventy. He steps down at seventy.

Garfinkle: Says who?

Coles: It's an agreement he has with the Board. His employment contract expires at seventy.

Garfinkle: The Board are his cronies. He is the Board. What he wants done gets done.

Coles: He gave me his word. He's a man of his word.

Garfinkle: Stop playing with yourself.

Coles: Twelve years ago he told me if I did the job it'd be my company to run when he steps down. That's why I came to that Godforsaken place. It's the same reason I'm here. I don't want the rug pulled out from under me so close to the finish line.

Garfinkle: You're wasting your time. I don't have two years.

Coles: Listen, Mr. Garfinkle. I said we could grow our other businesses by fifteen per cent. I was being conservative. We'll grow them in excess of twenty. I can manage. I can manage the hell out of a company. In two years we'll be worth considerably more.

Garfinkle: Billy boy, look at me. I weigh a ton. I smoke three packs a day. I walk from here to there, I'm out of breath. I can't even steal life insurance. Two years for me is forever. Do what you have to do now. I'm not a long term player.

Coles: I can't do it now. I can't do it till he leaves. If I try, I'm out on my ear.

Garfinkle: *(Handing* Coles *his briefcase.)* That's the problem with working for a living.

Coles: Two years is not a long time. I have waited a lifetime for the opportunity.

Garfinkle: *(Puts his arm around* Coles' *shoulder.)* You got stock, don't you?

Coles: Yes.

Garfinkle: Fifty, seventy-five thousand, right?

Coles: Sixty.

Garfinkle: Well, shit, look—want to feel better? (Garfinkle *taps out stock on his quote machine.)* Before you heard my name your stock was ten. Now it's fourteen and a half. In two months I made you a quarter of a million dollars. Billy boy, the least you can do is smile. Ossie at the bank sends me flowers. All I'm asking from you is a smile.

Coles *rises, takes his briefcase and silently moves Center Stage. He is alone. All else is black.*

Coles: Several years ago my doctor told me my right arm is three-fourths of an inch longer than the left. "How do I correct that?" I asked. "Carry the briefcase with your left arm for the next twenty-five years." *(Switches briefcase to the left arm.)* Charged me a hundred fifty dollars and wished me a good day.

Garfinkle: *(In the darkness.)* Smile, Billy boy, I just made you a quarter of a million dollars.

Coles: How come I like that doctor more than that pig? *(He turns and faces* Jorgenson's *darkened office.)* Jorgy, it's important.

Lights up in office as Jorgenson *rises to greet him.*

Jorgenson: Come on in. My door is always open. You know that.

Coles *enters.*

Welcome home. How was your trip to New York? How's Bill Jr.?

Coles: Fine.

Jorgenson: You must be exhausted. A day in New York is like a month anywhere else. Goddamned crazy city. Claire do any shopping?

Coles: Some.

Jorgenson: Only some? You got away lucky. Fay used to love to shop there—God rest her soul. Went to Bergdorf's Department Store, Lord and Taylor's Department Store, but she only bought at this Alexander's Department Store. She was a tight little so and so. Should've married Ossie.

Coles: She died the year before I got here. Jorgy—

Jorgenson: Last time we were in New York City was maybe . . . ten, fifteen years ago. We were in a taxicab on that highway coming in from the airport. Traffic? Nobody

moved for maybe half an hour. Cars standing still as far as
the eye can see. Suddenly some guy behind us went
"beep!" Next guy went "beep beep" a little louder. Before
you knew it there were these thousands of cars just parked
blaring away. Like an orchestra gone mad—just one giant
"beeeeep." Including my driver. You'd think he'd been
thrilled just sitting there on his ass with his foot on the
brake listening to that meter go tick, tick, tick.

Coles: I stopped by at Garfinkle's office.

Jorgenson: Let me just finish. You could hardly hear
yourself think. I shouted to the driver, "If you ever reach
the next exit turn around and take us back to the airport."
And that's exactly what he did. Fay didn't say a word.
Didn't have the nerve. That was the last time we were in
New York City ... and you know what was the most
amazing thing? It wasn't even rush hour.

Coles: He intends to take over the company.

Jorgenson: Say that again?

Coles: He intends to take over the company.

Jorgenson: He said that?

Coles: He didn't have to. A man with a gun in his hand
doesn't have to announce when he pulls the trigger. When
you find out, you're dead.

Jorgenson: What are you talking about? What gun?

Coles: He now owns eleven per cent of the stock.

Jorgenson: I have a million shares. That's twenty-five per cent. If he has a gun—I have a cannon.

Coles: And he's still buying.

Jorgenson: So would you. This is an undervalued company. Give him credit for recognizing that and putting his money where his mouth is. As it is it's turned out to be a pretty good investment for him. The stock's a lot higher now than when he started buying in.

Coles: Because he's the one moving it up.

Jorgenson: Don't be ridiculous. I'm not saying that's not a factor, but it's not the only one. Ossie told me he bought five thousand shares himself last week. And there are others.

Coles: You don't understand. He's well known. What he does is not a secret. He's called "Larry the Liquidator." on Wall Street. He finds companies worth more dead than alive, gains control and kills them. Then he pockets the proceeds and goes on to the next one. He spelled it out for us right here in this office. It couldn't have been any clearer.

Jorgenson: Suppose you're right. What would you like me to do? Last time I looked it was a free country.

Coles: We could do things to protect ourselves.

Jorgenson: Like what?

Coles: We could change our by-laws to call for a two-thirds majority to effect control rather than fifty-one percent.

Jorgenson: Would that make you feel better?

Coles: Of course it would. At least we'd be fighting back. We wouldn't be rolling over and playing dead.

Jorgenson: Nobody's playing dead. What you propose . . . what would it entail?

Coles: Not much. We'd have to change out state of incorporation from Rhode Island to Delaware.

Jorgenson: Delaware? I've never even been to Delaware.

Coles: Neither have I. We needn't be there. We needn't even visit there. All we'd have to do is hire a local lawyer and get a post office box.

Jorgenson: What would it cost?

Coles: One hundred and seventy-five thousand dollars for the first year. Fifty thousand dollars a year thereafter, for local counsel.

Jorgenson: Reclaiming the old stock and issuing the new?

Coles: About two hundred and fifty thousand. But that would be a one shot deal.

Jorgenson: For lawyers?

Coles: Primarily.

Jorgenson: Why can't we keep it a Rhode Island company?

Coles: It's easier to get those changes done in Delaware. They're—geared to corporate needs. And we'll show Garfinkle we're not a sitting duck. We intend to fight.

Jorgenson: By running away?

Coles: Running away?

Jorgenson: From Rhode Island to Delaware.

Coles: Nobody's running anywhere. It's a paper transaction.

Jorgenson: I call it running away. This company was founded in Rhode Island. It thrived in Rhode Island. It will remain in Rhode Island.

Coles: It will remain in Rhode Island. All that's moving is the paper.

Jorgenson: And the paper will remain in Rhode Island. Don't talk to me about playing dead. You know me better than that. Our industry is littered with dead bodies. This country is infested with dead bodies. But we're still here. And the lights go on and the telephone rings and orders come in and product goes out and we have money in the bank. And we didn't get there by playing dead.

Coles: At least talk to a lawyer.

Jorgenson: I am not talking to a lawyer. Lawyers are like cab drivers stuck in traffic. They don't do anything—but their meter is always ticking.

Coles: Please . . . just think about it.

Jorgenson: I have thought about it. Maybe you ought to think about something. I own twenty-five percent of this company. The Board owns another ten per cent. The employees' stock ownership plan five per cent. That's forty per cent. How is he going to get control?

Coles: From the sixty left.

Jorgenson: Please. They're long term holders. If they were looking to sell they would've sold when the stock was sixty. I'm sorry, I take your advice most of the time but in this instance you don't know what you're talking about.

Coles: I do know what—

Jorgenson: You are paid to manage this company. Manage it. It's my company. I'll see to it it stays that way, thank you.

Coles *pauses a beat, turns and moves Center Stage. Lights out on* Jorgenson.

Coles: "It's my company." Lord of the Manor with the House on the Hill ... How long do you work for something till it's finally yours?

Lights up on Garfinkle *in his office.*

Garfinkle: How long do you deliver the mail before they give you the post office? Billy boy, they don't give pots of gold to errand boys. They give pensions.

Coles: *(Whirling to* Garfinkle.) What?

Garfinkle: Talk to me. What's happening? How come I don't hear from you? What am I—a creditor?

Coles: I'm busy running a company, Mr. Garfinkle. What can I do for you?

Garfinkle: Talk to me. Have they broken ground on the Dunkin' Donuts next door?

Coles: I'm afraid not.

Garfinkle: That's disappointing. Got any more disappointing news? *(Long silence.)* . . . Helloooo.

Coles: How many shares do you own now, Mr. Garfinkle?

Garfinkle: You got a one-track mind. That's all you're ever interested in. Aren't you interested in me—my wife—my kids?

Coles: How are you, your wife, your kids?

Garfinkle: I'm not married. Never was. Don't have any kids. Who would marry me? . . . Come to think of it, you might. Shit, with my five hundred thousand shares we're engaged already. Bought the last this morning at fifteen and one eighth . . . hellooooo . . . Ossie at the bank stopped sending me flowers. Now it's plants. Looks like a fucking greenhouse in here—smells up the place. Have you talked to him?

Coles: I don't talk to Ossie.

Garfinkle: Not Ossie. Yorgy.

Coles: What about?

Garfinkle: Don't act stupid with me, Billy boy. It does

not become you—not to your fiancée. About restructuring.

Coles: Not yet.

Garfinkle: You intend to?

Coles: Yes.

Garfinkle: What are you waiting for?

Coles: The right opportunity.

Garfinkle: You figure that could occur in my lifetime?

Coles: I don't know, Mr. Garfinkle. I'm not your doctor.

Garfinkle: You got two weeks.

Coles: Two weeks?

Garfinkle: Talk to him. Get back to me. Otherwise I'll have to take a ride up there again. Believe me, you don't want to see that happen. I'm much less charming the second time.

Coles: Two weeks is unrealistic. I need—

Garfinkle: Two weeks. Say goodbye.

Coles: Mr. Garfinkle, two weeks—

Garfinkle: Say goodbye!

Lights out on Coles. Garfinkle, *breathing hard, turns and yells Offstage.*

Arthur—get the car ready. We're going back to the shitpit of the world. Bring donuts—and oxygen.

Lights out on Garfinkle. *Up on* Jorgenson's *office.* Coles *and* Bea *are seated.* Jorgenson *rises from behind his desk cheerfully.*

Jorgenson: Welcome, Larry, nice to see you again.

Garfinkle *enters.*

Garfinkle: Yumpin' yimminy, Yorgy, was that the sun I almost saw?

Jorgenson: It sure was. Come—look at it again. *(Leads him to the window. They stare out.)*

Garfinkle: Living up here is like living in a limo. You're always looking out through tinted windows.

Jorgenson: Larry, spring is here.

Garfinkle: Why not? It's been everywhere else.

Jorgenson: Come on. If a beautiful spring day doesn't bring out the sunshine in your soul, we'll have to—Bea, c'mon. Let's do it.

Bea: Now?

Jorgenson: Now. *(Bea exits, excited.)* Wait till you see this, Larry. I haven't even told Bill about it. *(Impatient, yells Offstage.)* C'mon, Bea. We're all waiting.

Bea: *(Offstage.)* Hold your horses, Jorgy. I'll be right there.

Jorgenson: Been with me for thirty-seven years. Yelled at me the same way back then.

Bea: *(Offstage.)* Ready?

Jorgenson: Ready. Ready.

Bea *enters pushing a stand-up rack on wheels filled with varying trays of donuts. Lots of them.*

C'mere—I'll show you how it works. *(He turns the handle on top and donuts move up and down like an old-fashioned toaster.* Garfinkle *quietly moves Center Stage, outside the office area, observing them.)*

Bea: Jorgy designed and built it this morning.

Jorgenson: Willard helped. He's our line foreman. And Kyle at the machine shop lent a hand. Larry, you're looking at a New England Wire and Cable product. Designed and built right here.

Bea: Keep turning.

Jorgenson: *(Continuing to turn handle.)* This lady drove all the way down to Providence this morning, almost thirty miles—sixty, round trip—to get them.

Bea: Closest Dunkin' Donuts I could find. Will you keep turning, Jorgy?

Garfinkle: With all the pricks in the world, I got to do business with a nice guy.

Bea: Look. Raspberry . . . toasted coconut.

Jorgenson: It comes apart. You could take it back to New York with you. A donut wheel for the donut man.

Bea: Chocolate sprinkles ... chocolate icing ... chocolate fudge ... chocolate cream ...

Garfinkle: *(Looking wistfully at the donuts.)* How unlucky can you get?

Jorgenson: Know the best part? Know who paid for the donuts? Ossie at the bank.

Garfinkle: ... Well, Ossie, ... it's you and me, Babe ... let's get to work.

Stage goes black. Pause a beat. Lights go back up in Jorgenson's *office. Everyone is there.*

Jorgenson: Larry, do me a favor. I'm a simple man. Restructuring, redeploying, maximizing—don't talk to me in Wall Street. Talk to me in English.

Coles: He wants you to sell the company.

Jorgenson: Is that what it's all about, Larry?

Garfinkle: *(To the tune of "Alfie.")* What's it all about, Larry?

Coles: Tell him. He won't believe me. Tell him.

Garfinkle: Not the company. Not the company. It's worth bupkus. You're lucky if you get the sixteen dollars a share it's selling at now.

Jorgenson: Then what, Larry? What do you want?

Garfinkle: I want what every other stockholder wants. I want to make money.

Jorgenson: You are making money.

Garfinkle: That's right. For all of us. I'm doing my part. Now you do yours.

Jorgenson: Do what? I don't have a printing press out there. I can't simply crank it out.

Garfinkle: Get rid of the Wire and Cable division. It's a financial cancer. And it's starving out all the other boring things Billy boy runs. Nobody sees them. All they see is the cancer.

Jorgenson: So you want me to sell Wire and Cable.

Garfinkle: Surgically remove it.

Jorgenson: To who, Mr. Garfinkle? Know anybody interested in buying a surgically removed cancer?

Garfinkle: I'll find you a buyer.

Jorgenson: Who?

Garfinkle: What's the difference?

Jorgenson: Who?

Garfinkle: Some paper shuffling Wall Street types. They'll give you a buck for every four you give them in equipment. I told you that.

Coles: And they'll close this down, and deduct it from their taxes.

Garfinkle: Easy. Just a paper transaction. Your hands won't even get dirty.

Jorgenson: And what happens to the plant?

Garfinkle: Gets sold for scrap.

Jorgenson: And the men? And the town?

Garfinkle: Not your problem. You're not the mayor. You're not a missionary.

Jorgenson: So that's what they mean when they talk about restructuring—maximizing shareholder values?

Garfinkle: That's what they mean.

Jorgenson: Nice turn of phrase. We used to call it "going out of business."

Garfinkle: Welcome to the wonderful world of Wall Street.

Jorgenson: Shouldn't surprise me. Those boys down there can't charge millions by going out of business. First they become lawyers and investment bankers—then they restructure.

Garfinkle: On Wall Street, "Restructuring means never having to say you're sorry." Got it?

Jorgenson: I got it. Now you get it. I understand what you want. Thank you for coming.

Garfinkle: Yorgy, are you dismissing me?

Jorgenson: I have no time for this. I have a company to run.

Garfinkle: *(To* Bea.*)* Sweetheart, pass me a donut. *(She looks at him, uncertain.)* Come on, the chocolate cream.

Bea: Get it yourself.

Coles: Please leave before it becomes unpleasant.

Garfinkle: Unpleasant? How quaint—how antiseptic—how "New England."

Jorgenson: Get out before I physically throw you out.

Garfinkle: All right, forget the donut.

Jorgenson: *(Rising.)* Out!

Garfinkle: Don't get your bowels in an uproar. We're just doing business.

Jorgenson: Do it somewhere else. You're not welcome here.

Garfinkle: Now I'm going to tell you something. I don't like the way my company is being run. There is a goddamned fire raging out there and this whole industry is up in flames. And you call the Fire Department and who shows up? Nobody. Because they're all off in Japan and Singapore and Malaysia and Taiwan and every other shithole place where they're crazy about pollution. And they build factories over there and they stuff them full of little dedicated people who work for twelve cents an hour, ten hours a day, six days a week and then they go home at night and pray for their health so they can come back and do it again tomorrow. And while that goddamned inferno is raging you're out front tidying up, mowing the lawn, playing with your putz on my money.

Jorgenson: Now you listen to me. This plant was here before you were born and I promise you—it will be here long after you're gone. Its products helped build the roads, bridges and buildings throughout the face of New England. And I will not—do you understand me—will not have it commit suicide and kill these people and this town so you and your cronies can pocket the insurance money.

Garfinkle: Don't think of it as suicide. Think of it as euthanasia.

Jorgenson: Go back to those other parasites on Wall Street. Tell them to restructure somewhere else.

Garfinkle *moves out of the office towards Center Stage.* Bea *takes a donut from the bin and hurls it in his direction.*

Bea: Here's your lousy donut!

Jorgenson: *(Kicks over the bin. The donuts litter the floor.)* Here's all your lousy donuts! *(They laugh. She comes over and they hug.)* God damn it, Bea. It feels good to fight something other than imports for a change.

Lights out in Jorgenson's *office.* Garfinkle *is alone Center Stage.*

Garfinkle: Geez ... You'd think I was asking them for a loan.

Lights out on Garfinkle. *Stage is black.*

Kate: *(In darkness, laughing.)* Take over! *(Lights up on* Kate *alone Onstage as she talks to her unseen* Mother. Kate *is an attractive, sexy woman, about thirty-five.)* What's so funny? Taking over New England Wire and Cable is like taking over the psychiatric ward at Bellevue. It could be done, but who wants to ... Mother, I'm sorry if it was in poor taste. That's who I am ... well, why not take the money and run? You should have retired a long time ago. Now's your chance ... Because I'm busy ... Busy in like having no time.

Lights up on Bea—*Cross Stage.*

Bea: You can take one day off from Stanley Morgan and fly up here—

Kate: Morgan, Stanley.

Bea: Morgan, Stanley and fly up here and talk to us. Jorgy was always crazy about you.

Kate: I was never crazy about him.

Bea: I did not ask your opinion. I am stating that he would be more at ease speaking to you than some stranger. I expect you to give us a day.

Kate: ... All right. I'm booked solid through the month. One day early next month.

Bea: I'll expect you here tomorrow.

Kate: Tomorrow?

Bea: Tomorrow. Catch the early flight. Come to the plant. We'll all be here.

Kate: *(Sighs, resigned.)* ... Coming, Mother. *(Lights out on* Bea.*)* Why is it that a grown woman, a lawyer, an executive with a staff of thirty and a budget of eight million plus, responsible for making hundreds of decisions every day, can revert to a spineless infant every time she talks to her mother? *(Kate picks up briefcase and moves to* Jorgenson's *office. Lights go up there.* Bea, Coles, *and* Jorgenson *await.)*

Kate: I understand what you said, but I don't understand what you want. Do you want me to help you negotiate a deal with him?

Jorgenson: There is no deal to be made with him.

Kate: Have you tried?

Bea: We want him to go away.

Kate: He's got half a million shares. No one walks away from half a million shares.

Coles: What do you suggest?

Kate: I'm a lawyer. Lawyers don't like to go to court. You never know what can happen. I suggest you settle.

Jorgenson: Meaning?

Kate: The man is motivated by dollars. Make it worth his while to leave.

Coles: Greenmail. Done all the time. Let's explore it.

Jorgenson: *(Rising.)* Excuse me. If this discussion continues on this tack I am leaving. We are wasting our time. There is no deal to be made with predators. You kill them or they kill you.

Kate: I was asked what I suggested. It is not my company and it is not my decision. *(She begins to rise as well.)*

Bea: *(To* Kate.*)* Please, Kate, we want to explore our options. Help us defend ourselves.

Kate: *(Reluctantly sits.)* All right. Let's say, I'm not at this point recommending anything. Just going over what others in your position have done. "Exploring the options," Mother.

Lights up on Garfinkle *as he views, unseen by them, their meeting.*

Garfinkle: Wait till you hear this.

Kate: Traditionally, first thing, you hire some private investigators to see what dirt there is. We know some good ones. Hopefully, they'll find something that will make him go away.

Garfinkle: Aw, Kate, you can do better than that.

Bea: Do you think there's a chance? Hasn't he been investigated before?

Garfinkle: Investigated? I get sued or subpoenaed every week. I've become a professional witness.

Kate: It's unlikely we'll find anything. He's reasonably well known. I think the S.E.C. got him on a few technical violations.

Garfinkle: That's right, girly. You mug somebody— you're walking the streets the same day. You don't file just one of fourteen hundred bullshit forms, they want to put you away for ten years.

Coles: We should do it. We have nothing to lose.

Garfinkle: It's not his money. Us "stuckholders" will pay for it.

Jorgenson: Doesn't sound promising. We have better things to do with our money.

Garfinkle: That man's got class . . . or he's cheaper than shit.

Kate: Get the Board to authorize a search for a white knight.

Bea: White knight?

Kate: A protector. A larger company that will buy you out and allow you to do business the way you want. You know, someone to rescue the damsel in distress . . . a white knight.

Jorgenson: I don't know anyone like that.

Bea: *(To* Kate.*)* Do you?

Garfinkle: Of course she doesn't *(Smiles, pats his middle.)* You got to have the stomach for it.

Jorgenson: Next.

Kate: We can formulate a "shark repellent."

Bea: Come again?

Bea: The purpose of a "shark repellent" is to make yourself undesirable to an unwanted suitor, i.e., shark.

Bea: How would that work?

Garfinkle: Listen close. It's an education.

Kate: Take the most attractive part of the company— in this case I assume it's the non-wire and cable divisions— give someone, anyone—the option to buy that part of the business for a song. The option only gets triggered if and when anyone not presently on the Board acquires thirty per cent or more of the company's stock. Garfinkle buys more shares, the option gets triggered. He now owns a lot of shares that are worth considerably less than he paid for them.

Jorgenson: So do we. So do all the stockholders.

Kate: That's the risk. The hope is that the shark will go elsewhere to feed.

Garfinkle: Ingenious, isn't it? Next.

Jorgenson: Next.

Garfinkle: Mah *man!*

Kate: We could create a poison pill. It's a form of shark repellent, but one you might find more acceptable. Get the Board to authorize three million shares of preferred stock, one share for each share held by all but Garfinkle. If he gains control of thirty per cent or more, issue them for, say—a dollar a share.

Jorgenson: A dollar a share!

Coles: What a great idea. We'd make Garfinkle's shares worth less. We'd dilute them.

Jorgenson: We would be diluting ours as well. Book value and earnings per share would be halved.

Kate: Exactly. Once you swallow the poison pill you're no longer desirable. But you can still keep your business. To most everyone nothing has changed.

Garfinkle: Except the stuckholder. People get paid big money—honored people—pillars of the community—to sit and dream this shit up. You know what I said when I first heard it?

Jorgenson: That's legal?

Garfinkle: That's what I said.

Kate: So far.

Garfinkle: Would you believe it?

Kate: It's not new. I can give you a list of companies—household names—that have it in their corporate by-laws.

Garfinkle: If you or me tried it, they'd have us committed.

Jorgenson: How much would your firm charge for taking us on?

Kate: I don't know. That's not my department.

Jorgenson: Rough guess?

Kate: It would depend on how involved it got. If we were able to work it out peacefully and quickly—a million. Maybe two. If it turned out to be war, it could go to ten, twenty times that.

Jorgenson: Kate, your mother is the only assisstant I ever had. She is also the best friend I ever had. I remember clearly the day you were born. The whole plant shut down a full afternoon while we had birthday cake and celebrated. This whole plant . . .

Bea: Jorgy, please.

Jorgenson: And it is out of respect for that lady that I don't have you bodily thrown out of this office.

Garfinkle: Bravo, Yorgy!

Kate: I'm sorry you feel that way. I'm only telling you how corporations under attack defend themselves. Don't blame the messenger for the message.

Jorgenson: The messenger, as I hear it, is saying pay him off or self-destruct. Either way, pay me my fee.

Kate: It is not my fee. Unfortunately, I'm only an employee. *(Picking up her briefcase to leave.)* I'm sorry we wasted each other's time.

Jorgenson: Have your firm send me a bill. That way only our time will have been wasted. I trust it'll be for something less than a million dollars.

Kate: It will. This one is on the house. And as long as it's my nickel, I want to tell you something. You, as they say on the street, are "in play." Garfinkle put you there. And now, right this second, all over the country there sit all kinds of boring, dull little men, hunched over their IBM PCs, buried under mountains of 13-D filings, looking for an edge to make a buck. And some of their little mini-computers have already noticed an obscure over-the-counter stock with a sixty per cent move in the last six months. "What's this? How come? What's going on?" they mutter. And then they notice Garfinkle's 13-D and his half-million shares. And they don't have to know diddly-doo about wire and cable. They know Garfinkle and they ride the coattails.

Congratulations.You're now "in play" in the big leagues where the game is called hardball and winner takes all. So if you want to play Mr. High and Mighty, Mr. Righteous, Mr. Robert's Rules of Order, better go to work for the Peace Corps where you'll be appreciated because you won't have any company left here to run.

(Begins to exit, turns.) And the shame of it is I would be perfect for this deal. Garfinkle is a blatant sexist. I love blatant sexists. They're my meat. But I wouldn't work for you if you begged me. I like being associated with winners.

Lights out in Jorgenson's *office.*

Garfinkle: *(Fanning himself.)* Phew ... some piece of work. *(Lights out on* Garfinkle.*)*

Bea: How dare you talk to him that way.

Kate: Will you stop defending him? He is making the wrong decision. He will lose this company.

Bea: He is making the right decision. We will not lose this company.

Kate: We!? Since when is it "we"? He loses this company, he walks away with millions. You walk away with memories.

Bea: Don't you worry about me. I'm well provided for.

Kate: "Well provided for". You have running water and you think you're well provided for.

Bea: Why are we talking about my finances? What is this all about?

Kate: Anger. About thirty-five year's worth.

Bea: At whom?

Kate: At him. And you. And this God-awful company. It's your life. It always was. When he was happy, you were ecstatic. When he was depressed, you were distraught. When she died, you almost moved in. It was the talk of the town. With Dad keeping the dinner warm.

Bea: I loved him.

Kate: You were married, Mother.

Bea: Listen to me, Kate. In a life filled with rumors and gossip and sideways glances—I apologized to no one.

Don't expect it of me now. You won't get it. You were asked here as our attorney, not our judge. If you can't handle the position—leave.

Kate: Why in God's name did you ever marry Dad?

Bea: I was nineteen. He asked. I thought I loved him. Until one day, thank God, I walked through that door. And there stood the most beautiful, scared young man I had ever seen. Had on blue jeans and a red flannel shirt with the sleeves rolled up. Said he just became President. I remember thinking, "How peculiar for a President. This company'll never last." And then the magic words: "How about it, Miss. I'm ready to take a chance with you. Ready to take one with me?" *(Turns to* Kate.*)* Sometimes life presents us with very limited choices.

Kate: I know.

Bea: Like now.

Kate: I don't believe you.

Bea: He trusts you. Don't make us deal with strangers in three piece suits. Maybe we can't play the game the way you want us to—help us play our game the best we can.

Kate: Oh Mother, don't you think I want to? Going up against Garfinkle, he's the best. And I'm as good as he is. It's the career opportunity of a lifetime.

Bea: So?

Kate: So, I said I wouldn't. Even if he begged me.

Bea: He's not. I am.

Kate *pauses a beat, picks up her briefcase and crosses to her* Mother *on the way to* Jorgenson's *office. Looks back.*

Kate: Well, c'mon. (Bea *moves to her and they begin their exit.)*

Bea: And you'll do something about those fees? They're horrendous.

Kate: *(Laughing.)* Mom, don't push it. *(They exit. Lights up on* Garfinkle.)

Garfinkle: You know what kills me? I've done maybe seven—eight deals like this. Know who I negotiate with? Skinny little joggers with contact lenses all stinking from the same aftershave. Don't believe me? Ever seen an arbitrageur? Ugliest people on the face of the earth. They won't use her. You'll see. I never luck out with a broad like that. Excuse me, woman like that. I've been accused of being a "womanizer." That's someone who likes broads. I remember when that used to be a good thing . . . although when you cut through the "Woman's Lib" bullshit all it really means is you can't call them "sweetheart" or "darling" unless you're schtupping them . . . . . . then you can't call them anything else. *(Sits behind his desk, smiles.)* I can live with that. (Kate *enters his office. Hands him her business card.)*

Kate: That's me. We're the investment banker for New England Wire and Cable.

Garfinkle: *(Looking at card.)* What are you—a fucking lawyer?

Kate: *(Smiling.)* Depends on who I'm with.

Garfinkle: *(Rises—opens arms—beams.)* Welcome to my life!

Kate: All those cubby-holes have lawyers in them?

Garfinkle: Mostly. *(She gives him a sad look.)* It's not as bad as you think. I don't have to talk to them. I just have to pay them.

Kate: You don't talk to them?

Garfinkle: Talk to them? I'd rather talk to my mother. I write to them. *(Takes top sheet from pile on desk. Writes.)* "Fuck ... them." *(Looks at* Kate.) Sue. *(Picks up next sheet. Writes.)* "Trouble." *(Looks at* Kate.) Settle. *(Picks up the next sheet. Writes.)* "They're ... morons." *(Looks at* Kate.) Let them sue. Don't give them a quarter. (Kate *laughs.)* See? Nothing to it. Sue. Settle. Defend. Which one are you?

Kate: I came to talk.

Garfinkle: Now that's trouble. Lawyers want to talk, it's nothing but trouble. Who are you? How come I never heard of you?

Kate: They generally keep me locked away at bond closings, due diligence meetings, good stuff like that.

Garfinkle: Life in the fast lane.

Kate: I'm not complaining. They pay well. I meet a lot of people. (Garfinkle *yawns.)* Well ... it's true. They don't have your ... something.

Garfinkle: *(Opening desk drawer.)* Want a donut?

Kate: No, thanks.

Garfinkle: Why not—you a health food freak?

Kate: No. Just not hungry.

Garfinkle: *(Incredulous.)* You have to be hungry to have a donut?

Kate: . . . You don't?

Garfinkle: Are you shitting me? In all my life I never heard of such a thing. Have to be hungry? Why? It don't taste better that way.

Kate: How would you know?

Garfinkle: My luck. A broad with a mouth.

Kate: Show me a broad worth knowing who doesn't have one.

Garfinkle: *(Laughs.)* I like you. Can you tell?

Kate: Not yet.

Garfinkle: Hang in. You will.

Kate: That's what I came to see you about. I need a month to hang in.

Garfinkle: Get lost.

Kate: I just got involved. I need time to get everybody's act together.

Garfinkle: My act is together.

Kate: If you give me some time I think we can work something out.

Garfinkle: Settle?

Kate: Work something out.

Garfinkle: I only settle when I'm in trouble.

Kate: Or when it makes sense.

Garfinkle: It only makes sense when I'm in trouble.

Kate: If you prefer, we'll go to court, get an injunction, have a fight, all kinds of allegations, cost them, cost you, and for what?

Garfinkle: I live in court. You got to do better than that.

Kate: . . . I won't love you any more.

Garfinkle: You got two weeks.

Kate: Standstill agreement.

Garfinkle: Both sides.

Kate: No more buying.

Garfinkle: Two weeks.

Kate: Thank you. *(Kate begins to exit.)*

Garfinkle: Now let's talk about what I want to talk about.

Kate: What's that?

Garfinkle: Your legs . . . your ass . . . your tits—

Kate: Sit. Sit!! *(He sits. She moves forward, her face close to his.)* Garfinkle, now listen close. I don't want to repeat this. You listening? Now take your right hand out of that donut drawer and put it between your legs. *(He looks at her, uncertain.)* Come on. They visit each other all the time.

Garfinkle: *(He laughs . . . a little nervously.)* . . . Can't.

Kate: Why?

Garfinkle: I'm a lefty. *(Switches hands. Fumbles a bit.)*

Kate: Good. Now look directly down at the little guy and say—"You must behave yourself when you're in the presence of a lady."

Garfinkle *sits motionless, transfixed.*

Garfinkle, if you don't say exactly that, right now, I'm resigning from this case. You'll deal with the Morgan Stanley "B" team. They think arbitrageurs are fun. *(He remains motionless. She rises, begins to exit.)*

Garfinkle: All right. All right.

Kate: "You must behave yourself when you're in the presence of a lady."

Garfinkle: ... "You must—" *(Kate motions him to put his chin on his chest. He does.)* "You must behave yourself when you're in the presence of a lady."

Kate: See, not so hard. *(He does a doubletake. She rises to exit.)* Hey, Garfinkle, what kind of donuts you got in that drawer?

Garfinkle: The good kind.

Kate: Toss one over. *(He reaches into drawer.)* With the right hand. See you in two weeks. *(He switches hands and tosses one over. She catches it and exits. He rises, takes a step or two Downstage, his voice filled with wonder.)*

Garfinkle: ... I think I'm falling in love ... *(Lights out on Garfinkle—up on Kate as she munches donut.)*

Kate: The man does have ... a certain undeniable ... charm.

Lights up in Jorgenson's *office.* Jorgenson, Coles, *and* Bea *await.*

Bea: Charm? He has as much charm as a beached whale.

Kate: *(Entering office.)* Don't knock it. It bought us two weeks.

Jorgenson: For what?

Kate: For getting our act together.

Jorgenson: What did it cost?

Kate: A donut.

Coles: Where do we go from here?

Kate: *(To* Jorgenson.*)* Have you reconsidered the defenses we spoke about?

Jorgenson: We won't do that.

Kate: Can I threaten it?

Jorgenson: I don't make threats I won't fulfill.

Kate: It's probably too late in the game for that anyway. Here's what you can do. Get the Board together. Authorize the purchase of as many shares as you can afford. Do it right away.

Jorgenson: The dollars we have are our safety net. Most of it is earmarked for future expansion.

Kate: Then borrow the money.

Coles: We have excellent credit. There's a dozen banks happy to lend us the money. It would be no problem.

Jorgenson: It's never a problem borrowing money. It's only a problem paying it back. *(To* Kate.*)* What would that do?

Kate: Three things. One: For every share you acquire it's one less Garfinkle can get. Two: and more important, you'll drive the price of the stock up. Eighteen sounds terrific when the stock is ten. Twenty is not so terrific when the stock is eighteen. The more it costs, the more negotiable he becomes. Get the stock up.

Jorgenson: I understand what you're saying. I'm not

sure I want to do that. We've been debt free since the Depression. It's what's permitted us to survive.

Kate: And it's that gorgeous balance sheet that also makes you so attractive—which is the third reason to buy the shares.

Jorgenson: What a strange new world. A strong, liquid balance sheet is no longer an asset. It's a liability.

Kate: Next, get a letter out to the shareholders. Tell them how great business is and how wonderful the future looks. Tell them how pleased you are that the investment community is finally beginning to recognize, in some small way, the real worth of the company. Thank them for their loyalty and support. Talk to as many of the larger shareholders as you can, personally. Under no circumstances mention any potential takeover.

Bea: I'll compile a list of everyone with more than five thousand shares.

Jorgenson: I don't need a list. I know who they are.

Kate: You have any political clout?

Bea: We're friendly with the Mayor and City Council.

Kate: Forget them. Too small. Do you have a relationship with the Governor?

Bea: Are you joking? He's a Democrat.

Kate: That's OK. I'll set it up from New York. We'll get some of our legislative people up there to talk to him. Prepare a statistical analysis of your dollar contribution to the local economy: jobs, payroll, taxes, etc. Make it as complete as possible.

Coles: You'll have it Monday.

Kate: Maybe we can get some anti-takeover legislation passed—quickly.

Coles: I don't mean to be crass . . . but . . . shouldn't we deal with something called . . . "golden parachutes"?

Bea: Golden parachutes?

Kate: You're premature. Don't muddy the water. We'll have time for that later.

Jorgenson: I think you've given us enough to tackle for the moment. We still have a business to run.

Kate: I agree. The important thing now is to get the stock up. I'll coordinate everything else. *(Begins to exit.)*

Jorgenson: Before you go, will you answer the question I asked you earlier?

Kate: What's that?

Jorgenson: Why did he give us two weeks? What did it cost?

Kate: *(Smiling.)*   . . . I told you—a donut. Chocolate fudge with sprinkles. *(Kate exits. Jorgenson moves Center Stage. Lights go out in his office.)*

Jorgenson: Donut, my ass. Garfinkle would never give two weeks. He'd sell them.

Bea: Jorgy, what the hell is a "golden parachute"?

(Lights go out on Jorgenson *and* Bea. Kate *screams in the darkness.)*

Kate: You son-of-a-bitch! You goddamned son-of-a-bitch! *(Lights up in* Garfinkle's *office.* Kate *enters. Flings papers at him.)* Goddamned hypocrite liar!

Garfinkle: But, sweetie-pie . . . but, honey-lamb—

Kate: We had an agreement. You gave me your word.

Garfinkle: But, baby-poo—

Kate: Stop that. You lied to me.

Garfinkle: Me?

Kate: We had a standstill. No more buying.

Garfinkle: So?

Kate: So? What's this tender to buy New England Wire and Cable at twenty dollars a share all about?

Garfinkle: Not me.

Kate: I bet. *(Picks up papers.)* OPM holdings—you know nothing about it?

Garfinkle: OPM? Not a lot to know.

Kate: I'm sure. . . . Where's the money coming from—junk bonds?

Garfinkle: Through Drexel. Give them fifteen per cent plus a fee and they'll get you the bucks to buy a slag heap in Mound City, Missouri.

Kate: Why did you have to lie to me? You embarrassed me with my firm. You embarrassed me with my clients.

Garfinkle: *(Slams his hand on desk. The ferocity of the blow startles* Kate.*)* Enough! Who am I dealing with here—Mother Teresa? Don't come on so goddamned holy with me, girly. You think I'm a fool—I sit here and twiddle my thumbs while you drive the price of the stock up?

Kate: I did no such thing.

Garfinkle: You're full of shit. All the buying was coming from some cock-a-mamie little brokerage firm in Rhode Island.

Kate: I know nothing about it.

Garfinkle: Give me a break, will you? That cheapskate is so tight he won't even put paint on the walls. The only way he'd be paying seventeen for his stock is if someone stood behind him with a cattle prod. Now I got as good an imagination as most but I tell you it's tough picturing Mother Teresa with a cross in one hand and a cattle prod in the other. *(Kate begins to leave.)* Don't go, Katie. I'm not through. You want to play the game—let's play. Only I don't watch while you do "holier than thou." That's not the way this game is gonna get played.

Kate: Game, huh?

Garfinkle: Goddamned right. The best game in the world.

Kate: You're playing Monopoly with people's lives here.

Garfinkle: I'm doing them a favor. I'm making them money. I thought that's what they were in the business for.

Kate: I know this might be difficult for you to believe—for some people business means more than making money. They don't know how to play your game.

Garfinkle: I'll teach them. It's easy. You make as much as you can for as long as you can.

Kate: And then what?

Garfinkle: And then what? Whoever has the most when he dies—wins.

Kate: Goodbye, Garfinkle.

Garfinkle: Aw, Katie, don't leave so soon. We haven't spoken about your thighs, your nipples, your—

Kate: See you in court.

Garfinkle: At least have a donut.

Kate: Stuff it.

Garfinkle: *(Downstage Right.)* You didn't have to leave. I'm not mad at you. Lying to protect your client is just doing your job good.

Kate: Round One to the fat man. It ain't over till it's over, fat man.

Garfinkle: And you didn't even ask what OPM stands for. *(With a big smile.)* "Other People's Money."

CURTAIN.

ACT TWO

Kate *with champagne bottle in hand in* Jorgenson's *office.* Jorgenson, Coles, *and Bea are standing expectantly.*

Kate: To Judge Pollard.

Bea: Judge Jim Pollard? For what?

Kate: For granting us an injunction preventing Garfinkle from buying more shares. *(They cheer, delighted.)*

Coles: A permanent injunction?

Kate: No. Pending the results of a suit we filed in Washington with the S.E.C. But since our Annual Meeting is in five weeks, for the purposes of taking control at that time, you could consider it permanent.

Coles: No more buying?

Kate: No more buying. He'll look to overturn it but he doesn't have time.

Jorgenson: Not with Jim Pollard presiding. Used to play football together in high school. Slowest son of a bitch on the team.

Kate: Didn't move slowly here. Granted us the injunction in two hours.

Garfinkle: *(Sings.)* "Territory folks should stick together."

Kate: Our legislative people met yesterday with the Governor and his Secretary of Commerce to discuss immediate anti-takeover legislation. They seem, I am told, very sympathetic.

Garfinkle: *(Sings.)* "Territory folks should all be pals."

Kate: I want to organize bus trips to the state capitol.

Get the workers, management, local politicians, everyone in town up there to see the legislators. And demonstrate, demonstrate, demonstrate.

Garfinkle: *(Sings.)* "Cowboys dance with the farmer's daughters."

Kate: I want to see babies. I want to see balloons. I want to see "Save Our Town, Save Our Future" posters hung from every school, church, bank and whorehouse in this city. I want visibility. I want prayer meetings. I want pressure!

Garfinkle: *(Sings.)* "Farmers dance with the rancher's gals!"

Lights fade in Jorgenson's *office.* Kate *moves Center Stage.*

Kate: God save me . . . I love this!

Lights up in Garfinkle's *office as he screams at his unseen staff.* Kate *looks on in amusement.*

Garfinkle: Seventeen lawyers on my payroll. Three goddamned law firms on retainer. And all of you together ain't worth some broad wet behind the ears. Some crew— you managed to work it out so in a free market in a free country I can't buy some shit-ass stock that every other asshole can buy. Congratulations. You know what? You— all of you—are destroying the capitalist system. And you know what happens when capitalism is destroyed? The Communists take over. And you know the one good thing that happens when the Commies take over? The first thing they do is kill all the lawyers!! And if they miss any of you—I'll do it myself.

Kate, *moving into his office, applauds.*

You liked it?

Kate: Loved it.

Garfinkle: The Wall Street version of "Let's win one for the Gipper."

Kate: It was wonderful. It's a shame Judge Pollard couldn't hear you.

Garfinkle: Stop gloating. It doesn't become you. What do you want?

Kate: A donut.

Garfinkle: *(Mimicking her.)* It's too early to be hungry.

Kate: *(Mimicking him.)* You have to be hungry to have a donut?

Garfinkle: *(Tossing her a donut.)* I see gloating is good for the appetite.

Kate: Who would know better than you?

Garfinkle: My luck. I meet a broad ... sweet, nice, Irish. In two weeks she turns into Don Rickles.

Kate *laughs.*

I like it when you laugh. You laugh nice.

Kate: You have the most incredible sense of humor. You make me laugh.

Garfinkle: Uh-oh. Here it comes. I'm in trouble.

Kate: *(Flirtatious.)* Let's be friends. Let's work it out. Let's settle.

Garfinkle: You've been eating too many donuts.

Kate: You only settle when you're in trouble. I thought I heard, "I'm in trouble."

Garfinkle: Only with you. You're wet behind the ears. I want you wet between your legs.

Kate *chokes on her donut.*

Aha—gotcha.

She nods, still choking.

Nice to see a girl blush nowadays. *(He moves behind her, gently and awkwardly patting her back as one would a child.)*

Kate: . . . Not blushing . . . choking.

Garfinkle: . . . Are you all right?

She nods.

Good. I don't want you to sue Dunkin' Donuts. The only thing better than their donuts is their stock.

Kate: Now that you almost killed me, can we talk?

Garfinkle: Talk. I'm listening. Just don't die on me.

Kate: What do you want to go away?

Garfinkle: . . . What do you mean?

Kate: What number do we buy you out at?

Garfinkle, *feigning horror, pretends to draw drapes, check for bugs, etc.*

What are you doing?

Garfinkle: Greenmail! Are you offering me greenmail?

Kate: Will you stop it?

Garfinkle: Are you?

Kate: Stop acting like it's new to you. You've done it three times in the past.

Garfinkle: I've done shit in the past. I don't play that way. It was never my idea. *(Talking into her briefcase.)* And I want the record to show it's not in this case either.

Kate: Why are you so uptight about it? It's not illegal.

Garfinkle: No, it's not. It's immoral. That distinction has no relevance for you lawyers—but it matters to me.

Kate: For someone who has nothing nice to say about lawyers you certainly have enough of them around.

Garfinkle: You have to. They're like nuclear warheads. They have theirs so you need yours—but once you use them they fuck everything up. They're only good in their silos.

Kate: *(Laughs.)* I'll have to remember that.

Garfinkle: Let me ask you something. You have authorization to offer me greenmail? . . . Bet your ass you don't. The others didn't either. It only comes from the lawyers. It's a lawyer's scheme. Everybody walks out happy. I get paid off. You get paid off. Yorgy keeps his company. Billy boy keeps his inheritance. The employees keep their jobs. Everybody comes out.

Kate: Sounds pretty good to me.

Garfinkle: Except the stuckholders. Their stock falls out of bed. They won't know what hit them.

Kate: I don't believe this. We better stop hanging out together. I turn into Don Rickles and you turn into Albert Schweitzer.

Garfinkle: Not Albert Schweitzer—Robin Hood. I'm a modern-day Robin Hood. I take from the rich and give to the middle class. Well . . . upper middle class.

Kate: Can we be serious now?

Garfinkle: I am serious. I really believe that . . . So what's your number?

Kate: The stock is eighteen. We'll buy it back at eighteen.

Garfinkle: First you laugh at me and then you insult me.

Kate: Why? Who else you know would buy a million shares of New England Wire and Cable at eighteen?

Garfinkle: Me. I'll pay twenty for them.

Kate: You can't. You got trouble.

Garfinkle: No trouble. Just delay.

Kate: I could maybe . . . get them to stretch to twenty.

Garfinkle: Now, why would I sell you something at the same price I was willing to pay for it?

Kate: Your average cost was thirteen. Thirteen from twenty, times a million, isn't a bad day's pay on one little deal.

Garfinkle: I'm not interested in seven million. I'm interested in value. The value here is no secret. I spelled it out for them. I was being conservative.

Kate: Spell it out for me. What's the number?

Garfinkle: Twenty-five.

Kate: Impossible.

Garfinkle: What's impossible—It's worth it or they'll

pay it?

Kate: Both. That stock hasn't seen twenty-five in ten years.

Garfinkle: You want history? That stock was once sixty. I was once skinny. . . . Well, skinnier.

Kate: Take twenty.

Garfinkle: Take a walk. Twenty-five is my number. And that's a favor.

Kate: I can't deliver that.

Garfinkle: I know. Let's talk about something nice. Let's talk about your eyes.

Kate: *(Getting up to leave.)* I really thought we could work something out.

Garfinkle: We can't. You're too far away.

Kate: You could lose it all.

Garfinkle: I could. That's why so few of us have the balls to play the game.

Kate: Thanks for the donut.

Garfinkle: Don't be depressed. You're in a tough place. Go fight your fight. It's not personal—it's principle. Hey, no matter what—it's better than working at the post office.

Kate: *(Softly.)* Oh yeah ... It's better than the post office.

She smiles sadly and exits. He is alone.

Garfinkle: A lot better than working at the post office.

It's the best there is. Like in the old westerns, didn't everyone want to be the gunslinger? Didn't everyone want to be Butch Cassidy and the James Boys? There's just a few of us—us modern-day gunslingers. There's T. Boone and the Bass Brothers out of Texas. Irwin Jacobs out of Minneapolis. Would you believe a gunslinger named Irwin Jacobs? The Belzberg Boys up north in Canada. And here in New York we got Saul Steinberg and Ronny Perlman and Carl Icahn.— *(Places his hand on his heart.)* Out of respect for the stupid, a moment of silence for our gunned-down colleague Ivan Boesky. *(With a big smile.)* It's assholes like him that give assholes like us a bad name. And last, but not least, Garfinkle from the wilds of the Bronx. But instead of galloping in with a six gun a-blazing in each hand, we're driven in, escorted by a herd of lawyers and investment bankers, waving our limited partnerships in one hand and our 13-D filings in the other. But they quake just as hard. And they wind up just as dead. And it's legal. And it's exciting. And it's fun. *(Moves to desk.)* And the money ain't bad either. *(Sits at desk.)* And every so often, every once in a while, we even wind up with the girl. *(Begins looking at papers on desk. Looks up.)* It's a nice business.

As he works quietly for a beat, we hear Kate *shouting Offstage.*

Kate: What? What are you so hysterical about—interrupting my meeting. *(She enters his office.)* What the hell is so important? You having a stroke—a nervous breakdown?

Garfinkle: Just taking care of business.

Kate: You're worse than my mother.

Garfinkle: Please. I know we're on different sides here—

Kate: I'm busy. What's so important? What do you

want?

Garfinkle: I feel bad about our last meeting. You left, you looked so depressed. I want us to be friends. I want us to end our dispute. I have two propositions. I'll give them to you in my order of preference.

She sits.

Sure. If I was having a stroke you'd tell me to dial 911—Now you're ready to spend the afternoon. How about the evening?

Kate: Proposition number one?

Garfinkle: We leave here, right now, and go to my place where we make wild passionate love for the rest of the afternoon.

Kate: Number two?

Garfinkle: Wait a minute. I'm not finished. The first one who comes, loses.

Kate: Loses what?

Garfinkle: The deal. I come first I sell you back my shares at cost. I slink away never to be seen or heard from again. You come first, you tender all your shares to me at twenty.

Kate: You're serious?

Garfinkle: Well, I don't slink. Big men don't slink. I . . . saunter away. Are you interested?

Kate: How do you suggest we write this up for the proxy statement?

Garfinkle: Delicately. Under the heading easy come, easy go.

Kate: The garment center is too classy for you.

Garfinkle: Come on, what do you got to lose—your virginity? I could lose millions.

Kate: You've thought of everything!

Garfinkle: Not everything. What happens if we come together?

Kate: We call and make sure your life insurance premiums are paid. *(Kate moves out of office to Center Stage.)*

Garfinkle: Hey, premiums are paid.

Lights out on Garfinkle. Kate *is alone.*

Kate: You think he was serious? So help me, I don't know.

On the one hand, if he was serious . . . *(She laughs.)* We would have made Wall Street history . . . maybe. *(Moving to* Jorgenson's *office.)* And on the other hand, proposition number two is something to talk about.

Lights up in Jorgenson's *office.* Bea, Coles *and* Jorgenson *excitedly greet* Kate *as she enters.*

Don't get too excited. Don't break out the champagne. He gave me two propositions. Here's the one worth talking about. Inasmuch as Judge Pollard will not lift his injunction and inasmuch as his money is all tied up and inasmuch as your lawyer can be very persuasive, he's agreeable to swap you his shares for the Wire and Cable division.

Bea: . . . What?

Kate: He owns a million shares. He gives them to us. We give him the Wire and Cable division.

Coles: Makes sense. It costs him thirteen million for something he'll sell for thirty—thirty-five million.

Jorgenson: *(Trying to control himself.)* What are the alternatives?

Kate: Don't dismiss it so quickly. On Wall Street it's know as "restructuring." Look what happens. The losses at Wire and Cable disappear. The earnings of the other divisions surface. Your stock skyrockets.

Jorgenson: What are the alternatives?

Kate: Better yet, when you get back his million shares you absolutely control this company. It's yours. No one can take it away.

Jorgenson: I'm asking you for the last—

Kate: I can't play with him in the courts forever. Ultimately he gets the injunction withdrawn, buys more shares . . . don't you understand?

Bea: We're not stupid—we understand. What are the alternatives!

Kate: Greenmail. Poison pills. Restructuring. You choose. I have given you the alternatives.

Jorgenson: You've given me nothing but different ways to kill myself.

Coles: Jorgy, this idea works. We're rid of the losses. We're in total control. And our stock doubles.

Jorgenson: To hell with the price of our stock. I will not do Garfinkle's dirty work for him.

Kate: I'm pleading with you. I'm imploring you.

Jorgenson: I will not do it. I will not kill these people and this town to enrich the man who is trying to destroy me.

Kate: You're a fool. You're a neanderthal. You deserve to lose this company!

Bea: Stop that. This is not a chess game. It's not simply a matter of tactics. What's the matter with you? This used to be your home. This is family.

Kate: Family!?

Bea: Yes. The kids you went to school with earn their livings at this plant. Family.

Kate: Oh, good God. Okay, let's talk about family. Let's start with Dad. Let's start with his dreams and his family.

Bea: Your father is dead. But we're not dead. And this plant is not dead. And our dreams aren't over and they'll never end with greenmail and poison pills.

Kate: Stop talking dreams. Look at the reality.

Bea: I am looking at the reality and I don't like what I see. It scares me. Who are you, Kate? What ever happened to that brave young girl who set out to do battle to heal all the world's ills? *(Distraught.)* What ever happened to my baby?

Jorgenson *moves to* Bea. *With his arm around her shoulder, he begins ushering her off.*

Jorgenson: Please.

Bea: What are you doing? She is my daughter. This is my fight.

Jorgenson: This is our company. This is my fight, too. I won't embarrass you. Promise.

Bea *reluctantly exits.* Kate *begins to leave.*

Hold on a minute ... What do you want of me, Kate?
Want me to say "I'm sorry"? For what? For loving your
mother? I'm not. Look, we are fighting for our lives—here
and now ... Why are we even talking about this?

Kate: Because it still hurts.

Jorgenson: What do we do now, Kate? Go over
it—resolve thirty-some odd years of hurt in the next
fifteen minutes? Is that what you expect?

Kate: No, I don't. But I'll tell you what I do expect. I
expect not to be lectured to about "family" by my mother
and I expect not to be abused by you.

Jorgenson: Abused?

Kate: I turned my life upside down to come up here to
help you out. I don't even get to take off my jacket and
you're ready to have me "bodily thrown out of your
office." Well, I'll make it easy for you. I'll leave. *(She turns
to exit.)*

Jorgenson: Well, go ahead then and leave. You're a
lousy lawyer anyway.

Kate: I am a lousy lawyer!? I want to tell you something.
I'm a goddamned good lawyer. You are a lousy client. You
say "No" to everything. You say "No" to what ninety-nine
percent of other corporations say "Yes" to. If this was any
other outfit they'd put a statue out there in the yard of the
woman that saved this company.

Jorgenson: Saved this company? You're not looking to
save this company. You're looking to save your own ass.

Kate: ... What?

Jorgenson: Being beaten by Garfinkle wouldn't look so

good on your resume, would it? Damn it, Kate—you want to win so badly, you don't even know what this fight is all about!

Kate: Oh, yes, I do. It's about your incredible—pigheadedness.

Jorgenson: Okay. Sure it is. But it's also about the twelve-hundred men who work here and their families—and their future. Let's ask them if you're trying to "save this company."

Kate: Why ask them? They're not stockholders.

Jorgenson: Does that mean they don't matter?

Kate: ... Okay ... Look. They matter. Nothing gets resolved but everything matters.

Jorgenson: What matters most is this is my nickel. So let's stop fighting about what I won't do and let's start fighting about what I will do.

Kate: Okay. Here's my problem. I'm a good lawyer. I'm a lousy mindreader. What will you do?

Jorgenson: I'll leave it up to the stockholders.

Kate *laughs.*

Kate: You will leave it up to the stockholders?

Jorgenson: They haven't let me down yet.

Kate: They haven't met Garfinkle yet.

Jorgenson: I don't have a choice. I do—not—have a choice I can live with.

Kate: Oh, why couldn't you be an asshole like everybody else?

Jorgenson: I'm sorry. I thought I was doing my best.

Kate: This 40% ... This faithful 40% ... Can you absolutely count on it?

Jorgenson: Absolutely. Come on, let's kick his ass all the way back to Wall Street.

Kate: Jorgy, if I play Garfinkle right. If I massage that ego just right, this could work!

Kate *and* Jorgenson *move into* Jorgenson's *office.* Coles *enters alone.*

Coles: It didn't seem the appropriate time to ask: "And what happens to me if we lose?" It never seemed the appropriate time to ask that. When you spend your life managing a business you're trained to think in contingencies. What happens if sales don't meet expectations? What happens if costs go up—the economy down? What happens if ...

So ... later that afternoon, with a lump in my throat, I asked, "What happens to me if we lose? I deserve," I said, "a golden parachute. Managements with far worse records than mine routinely give themselves at least five years' pay. It's done all the time. And it wouldn't cost you anything." ... Know what he said?

Jorgenson: *(In his darkened office.)* Up here we don't plan the funeral until someone dies.

Coles: Isn't that something?

Coles *exits. Lights up in* Jorgenson's *office.* Kate *is preparing to leave.*

Jorgenson: So ... You think he'll go for it?

Kate: ... I don't know.

Jorgenson: You can do it. Use some of that home grown New England charm. Talk nice. Smile sweet. You'll get him.

Kate: *(Exiting his office.)* Don't go away. *(Moves Downstage Center. Lights out on Jorgenson's office. She turns to Garfinkle's darkened office.)* Hey Garfinkle!

Lights go up on Garfinkle in his office.

Rumor has it you got balls.

Garfinkle: I've been trying to show you for weeks.

Kate: Show me now. Let's leave it up to the stockholders. Run your own slate of directors at the Annual Meeting. You get 51% of the votes, it's your company. You buy everybody out at twenty. You don't get the votes, you sell us back your shares at thirteen. You slink away, never to be seen or heard from again . . . What do you say, Garfinkle? Hardball. Winner takes all.

Garfinkle: Is that what you want?

Kate: A lot.

Garfinkle: I don't know. It's a tough proposition. You control 40% of the votes going in.

Kate: What do you got to lose? On a worst case basis you come out even. It only cost you thirteen.

Garfinkle: I don't know. It's gonna be close.

Kate: Robin Hood makes the deal.

Garfinkle: . . . Yeah. Do it.

Lights out on Garfinkle's office. Kate turns to Jorgenson's office. Lights come up. Bea and Jorgenson are present.

Kate: Done. *(She moves to exit.)*

Jorgenson: Hold on. Where are you going?

Kate: The airport.

Jorgenson: I'll give you a lift.

Kate: Don't bother.

Jorgenson: At least let me tell you how great you did.

Kate: We'll see at the Annual Meeting.

Bea: I know this wasn't your preference. Thanks for sticking your neck out. How does it feel?

Kate: Scary. It's going to be close.

Jorgenson: Close? We have forty percent. He has twenty-five. We would only need ten of the remaining thirty-five. That's less than one in three. If we can't get that—Christ, Richard Nixon could get that.

Bea: *(To Kate.)* Always wanted to be a politician.

Jorgenson: I did. Always wanted to be Harry Truman. Goddamned son of a bitch just went out and told the truth. *(To Bea.)* And that's what we're going to do. We're going out there and tell the truth. Send a letter to the stockholders? We'll visit them. Hell, we'll even have them over for dinner.

Kate: Harry and Bess hit the campaign trail. *(Begins to leave.)*

Jorgenson: Before you go. You said he gave you two propositions. What was the other?

Kate: Oh, just Garfinkle's idea of a tender offer. Come on. Drive me to the airport.

Blackout. Lights up on Garfinkle *alone in his office.* Coles *enters, briefcase in hand.)*

Garfinkle: Aw, Christ—What do *you* want?

Coles: Good morning, Mr. Garfinkle.

Garfinkle: Are you about to regale me with the latest saga of Bill Jr. at Columbia?

Coles: Strictly business, Mr. Garfinkle. As you know, I had sixty thousand shares of New England stock when we first met.

Garfinkle: Excuse me—it'll be a history lesson instead.

Coles: Since becoming aware of your investment I have purchased an additional forty thousand shares. I now have a hundred thousand.

Garfinkle: Congratulations.

Coles: I'm prepared to sell you the right to vote those shares at the Annual Meeting. Are you interested?

Garfinkle: Sit down. I'm interested.

Coles *sits.*

How much?

Coles: A million.

Garfinkle: Too much.

Coles: You need a million shares above what you own. I can get you ten percent of the way there in one transaction. Better yet, it's votes they're counting on for themselves. I think what I'm asking is fair.

Garfinkle: If your shares make a difference—if I win by

less than a hundred thousand—Otherwise I don't need them. I won't vote them.

Coles: I'm not selling you an option. I'm selling you the right to vote the shares. How you vote them, if you vote them, is your business. It's of no concern to me.

Garfinkle: . . . If they make the difference, you got your million. If they don't, half a million.

Coles: Agreed. *(Reaching into his briefcase.)* I've prepared the papers. I just left the numbers blank. Have your lawyers review it. I'm staying over. I'll pick it up in the morning—along with a check. *(Places papers neatly on Garfinkle's desk.)* Good day, Mr. Garfinkle.

Coles *exits* Garfinkle's *office. Moves Center Stage.* Garfinkle *shouts after him, a beat after his exit.*

Garfinkle: And how is Bill Jr. doing with his studies?

Garfinkle *moves his clenched fist through the air in celebration. Lights out on* Garfinkle. Coles *is alone.*

Coles: Don't look at me like that. Everybody looks out after their own self-interest. "What's in it for me?" Isn't that, ultimately, what it's all about? Jorgenson looks out for his monument. Garfinkle for his money. Bea for her man. Kate for her career. The employees for their paycheck. I kept this company alive. I helped make it all possible. Who looks out for me? *(Coles hurriedly exits. Lights up on* Bea *as she tries to get her bearings.)*

Bea: This way? . . . Through there . . .

Lights up on Garfinkle *in his office. She enters.*

Good afternoon, Mr. Garfinkle.

Garfinkle: Oh, no—the donut thrower. Wait—I got to

get my catcher's mask.

Bea: I'm sorry. I didn't bring any.

Garfinkle: Aw . . . And I was looking forward to some of your nutritious health donuts—you know—yogurt sprinkles—penicillin-filled.

Bea: . . . These offices are every bit as impressive as my daughter said they were.

Garfinkle: . . . What do you know . . . I like your daughter. She's hot shit.

Bea: . . . I think so, too . . . assuming I know what you mean.

Garfinkle: You know what I mean. She's terrific. And she didn't get that way working for those clowns at Morgan, Stanley. She must've got it from you.

Bea: That's kind of you.

Garfinkle: Did she send you? I wouldn't put it past her.

Bea: She didn't send me. She would be upset with me if she knew. I expect this meeting will be held in confidence.

Garfinkle: Have a seat.

She sits.

What can I do for you?

Bea: You can take the million dollars I'm about to offer you.

Garfinkle: *(Sitting.)* . . . This is gonna be some day.

Bea: I thought that might interest you. There is a trust fund, in my name, with a million dollars, primarily in treasury notes, in it. I will turn it over to you if you call off your fight with us. We will buy back your shares at thirteen, which Kate informs me gets you even, plus you'll have a million dollars profit.

Garfinkle: How come I never had a mother like you?

Bea: Is that acceptable?

Garfinkle: My mother—I gotta send a check once a month. Would you like to meet her?

Bea: Is that acceptable?

Garfinkle: How much money you make a year?

Bea: I don't see—

Garfinkle: How much?

Bea: Forty thousand. Plus health insurance.

Garfinkle: Why would you give up a million to save forty?

Bea: That's my affair. Is it agreeable to you?

Garfinkle: Who are you doing it for?

Bea: Myself. I don't need the money.

Garfinkle: I don't either.

Bea: Then why are you doing it?

Garfinkle: That's what I do for a living. I make money.

Bea: You will have made money. If you accept my offer you will have made a million dollars. For a few weeks' effort you will have made more than most working a lifetime.

Garfinkle: Go home. I don't want your money.

Bea: Why? Isn't it good enough for you?

Garfinkle: It's good. It's just not enough.

Bea: I know a million dollars is not a great deal of money to you. It's all I have. If I had more I'd give you more. I had really hoped to appeal to whatever decent instincts you have left. I'm here to plead for my company.

Garfinkle: Go home.

Bea: Please, Mr. Garfinkle.

Garfinkle: I don't take money from widows and orphans. I make them money.

Bea: Before or after you put them out of business?

Garfinkle: You're getting on my nerves. Go home.

Bea: I intend to. Before I go I'd like to know—I'd like you to tell me—how you can live with yourself?

Garfinkle: I have no choice. No one else will.

Bea: How? How can you destroy a company . . . its people . . . for the sake of dollars you don't even need?

Garfinkle: Because it's there.

Bea: . . . Because it's there?

Garfinkle: What? People climb mountains—swim oceans—walk through fire—'cause it's there. This way is better. You don't get all sweated up.

Bea: There are people there. There are dreams there—

Garfinkle: Do you want to give a speech or do you want an answer? 'Cause the answer is not complicated. It's simple. I do it for the money. I don't need the money. I want the money. Shouldn't surprise you. Since when do needs and wants have anything to do with one another? If they did I'd be back in the Bronx and you'd be getting Yorgy his coffee up in Grimetown. You don't need the job. You need the million dollars. But you're prepared to give up what you need—a million dollars—for what you want—a stinking job. You're fucked up, lady. You're sick. Go see a psychiatrist.

Bea: You are the sick one. Don't you know that?

Garfinkle: Why? 'Cause I know what I want and I know how to get it? Lady, I looooove money. I love money more than I love the things it can buy. And I love the things it can buy. You know why? Money is unconditional acceptance. It don't care whether I'm good or not, whether I snore or don't, which God I pray to—it still gets me as much interest in the bank as yours does. There's only three things in this world that give that kind of unconditional acceptance—dogs, donuts and money. Only money is better. It don't make you fat and it don't shit all over the living room floor.

Bea: I hope you choke on your money and die!

She exits. Garfinkle *smiles sadly.*

Garfinkle: How come I always bring out the best in people?

Lights up on Kate *Cross Stage.*

Kate: You bring out the best in me.

Garfinkle: I know I do. Katie, me girl.

Kate: The Irish in me.

Garfinkle: ... Same thing.

Kate: What's the matter? Are you becoming melancholy on me?

Garfinkle: Melancholy? Why would you say that? Just 'cause the Governor calls every hour ... the unions are picketing my house ... prayer meetings daily chant for my demise—

Kate: *(Moving toward him.)* You're in the wrong profession. You should head the U.N. Nobody can bring people together like you ... not even a chuckle? You must really be in bad shape. Feeling unloved?

Garfinkle: Unappreciated. I'm doing the right thing. I'm taking unproductive assets and making them productive. Just following the law of free enterprise economics.

Kate: What law is that?

Garfinkle: Survival of the fittest.

Kate: The Charles Darwin of Wall Street!

Garfinkle: *(Laughing.)* ... I like that. The Charles Darwin of Wall Street.

Kate: Maybe they don't see it that way. Maybe they don't see it as survival of the fittest. Maybe they see it as survival of the fattest.

Garfinkle: Aw, Katie, why are you so hard on me?

Kate: 'Cause you're not nice.

Garfinkle: Since when do you have to be nice to be right?

Kate: You're not right. You're "What's happening."

One day we'll smarten up and pass some laws and put you out of business. Ten years from now they'll be studying you at the Wharton School. They'll call it the "Garfinkle Era" and rinse out their mouths when they leave the room.

Garfinkle: That's how you talk about family?

Kate: Family?

Garfinkle: Immediate family. For every deal I find, you guys bring me ten. We happen to be in bed together, lady. Calling it family, that's being nice. Look at me, Kate.

Kate: I'm going to put you away, Garfinkle.

Garfinkle: I'm not going away. They can pass all the laws they want—all they do is change the rules—they can't stop the game. I don't go away. I adapt. Look at me, Kate. Look at you. God damn it! We're the same!

Kate: We are not the same. We are not the same! We sit on opposite sides here. I like where I sit. You sit in shit.

Garfinkle: You sit with me.

Kate: You sit alone.

Garfinkle: Alone? Get off it, will you? We've come from "Ask not what your country can do for you" to "What's in it for me?" to "What's in it for me—today!" all in one short generation. That's why those stockholders all love me and that's why you guys all work for me. Nobody's putting a gun to anyone's head. Everybody's got their hand out.

Kate: Not everybody. Not me. Not them.

Garfinkle: Forget them. It's about you and me, now, Kate. I'm the last thought you have when you fall asleep at night and the first when you wake in the morning. I make those juices flow and you know it.

Kate: Garfinkle, if you knew what you do to me you wouldn't brag about it.

Garfinkle: Bullshit. And you know what makes the two of us so special? What sets us apart? We care more about the game than we do the players. That's not bad. That's smart.

Kate: That's grotesque. Garfinkle, you don't know me at all. You're not capable of knowing me. You can't see beyond your appetite.

Garfinkle: Then what the fuck are you doing here!? You can't stay away. You don't want to stay away. Come— play with me. Be a player—not a technician. Feel the power. This is where you belong, Kate. With me. I know you. I know who you are. I like who you are. I want you, Kate.

He reaches for her. She pulls away.

Kate: I'm going to nail you, Garfinkle. I'm going to send you back to Wall Street with donuts up your ass and everyone's going to know how some broad wet behind the ears did you. And whatever happens from this day forward, whatever successes I achieve, none—none will be sweeter than this one!

She exits. Garfinkle, *a beat after the exit, yells to her.*

Garfinkle: You're so perfect for me! *(Turns, begins to exit.)* To be continued. In Grimetown.

He exits. Lights up on Jorgenson *alone in his office.* Bea *enters.*

Bea: Hey, good lookin', whatcha got cookin'. How's about cookin' something up with me?

He smiles weakly.

You okay?

Jorgenson: Just going over in my head what I want to say.

Bea: They're putting speakers out in the hallways. The auditorium won't fit everyone. I feel like we're Harry and Bess on election night.

Jorgenson: Harry was a better man than me. Went to sleep election night. I haven't slept good for days.

Bea: Talk to me.

Jorgenson: I'm scared, Bea. I'm scared time has passed us by. I'm scared I don't know this new environment. I'm scared what I do know doesn't count for anything any more.

Bea: *(Moves behind him. Rubs his neck.)* I'm not scared. I'm proud. I'm proud of the business we built. Most of all I'm proud of you. And if what we are counts for nothing anymore, that won't be our failing—it'll be theirs.

He smiles. Squeezes her hand.

It'll be all right. Just go out and tell the truth. Go out and give them hell, Harry.

They remain frozen. Garfinkle *enters. Looks at them.*

Garfinkle: The truth? Why don't you tell the truth, lady? The truth is Harry Truman is dead.

Lights dim on Bea *and* Jorgenson *though they continue visible.* Garfinkle *moves to his darkened office.* Bea *moves Downstage*

Center to a podium. We're at the Annual Meeting. Scene is played as if audience were the stockholders.

Bea: That concludes the formal aspect of our Annual Meeting. The one remaining item of business is the election of directors. Is there anyone entitled to vote who does not have a ballot? Please raise your hand. *(She looks about at the audience.)* Will the inspector of elections distribute the ballots? Please keep your hand raised so you can receive your ballot. Thank you.

Jorgenson *rises from his office and moves to lectern.*

Jorgenson: It's nice to see so many familiar faces . . . so many old friends . . . many of you I haven't seen for years. Thank you for coming and welcome to the 73rd Annual Meeting of New England Wire and Cable—the 38th of which I am addressing you as your Chief Executive.

Bill Coles, our able President, has told you about our year; what we accomplished—where we need to make further improvements—what our business goals are for next year and the years beyond.

I'd like to talk to you about something else. On this, our 73rd year, I'd like to share with you some of my thoughts concerning the vote you are about to make in the company you own.

We've had some very good years. We've had some difficult ones as well. Though the last decade has been troubling for us it's been devastating for our industry. Ten short years ago we were the twelfth largest manufacturer of wire and cable in the country, the fourth largest in New England. We're now the third largest in the country and the largest in New England.

We might not have flourished—but we survived. And

we're stronger for it. I'm proud of what we accomplished.

So, we're at that point where this proud company, which has survived the death of its founder, numerous recessions, a major depression and two world wars, is in imminent danger of self-destructing this day in the town of its birth.

And there is the instrument of our destruction. I want you to see him in all his glory. Larry the Liquidator—the entrepreneur in post-industrial America—playing God with other people's money.

Garfinkle *waves to stockholders. Sits once again.*

At least the robber barons of old left something tangible in their wake. A coal mine. A railroad. Banks. This man leaves nothing. He creates nothing. He builds nothing. He runs nothing. In his wake lies nothing but a blizzard of paper to cover the pain.

If he said, "I could run this business better." Well, that's something worth talking about. He's not saying that. He's saying, "I am going to kill you because at this particular moment in time you're worth more dead than alive."

Well, maybe that's true. But it is also true that one day this industry will turn. One day when the dollar is weaker or the yen stronger or when we finally begin to rebuild the roads, the bridges, the infrastructure of our country demand will skyrocket. And when those things happen we will be here—stronger for our ordeal— stronger for having survived. And the price of our stock will make his offer pale by comparison.

God save us if you vote to take his paltry few dollars and run. God save this country if *(Pointing to* Garfinkle.) "that" is truly the wave of the future. We will then have become a nation that makes nothing but hamburgers, creates nothing but lawyers, and sells nothing but tax shelters.

And if we have come to the point in this country where we kill something because at the moment it's worth more dead than alive, then turn around and take a good look at your neighbor. You won't kill him because it's called "murder" and it's illegal. This, too, is murder, on a mass scale, only on Wall Street they call it "maximizing shareholder values" and they call it legal and they substitute dollar bills where a conscience should be.

Damn it. A business is more than the price of its stock. It is the place where we make our living, meet our friends and dream our dreams. It is, in every sense, the very fabric that binds our society together.

So let us, right now, at this meeting, say to every Garfinkle in this land, that here we build things—we don't destroy them.

Here, we care for more than the price of our stock.

Here . . . we care about people!

Jorgenson *moves from lectern back to table.* Bea, Coles, and Kate *stand and applaud.* Garfinkle *follows* Jorgenson *back and as the applause dies, says to* Bea, Coles *and* Jorgenson *respectively:*

Garfinkle: Amen . . . And Amen . . . And Amen. Say "Amen," someone, please! *(Moves to lectern in and says in a hushed tone.)* You'll excuse me. I'm not familiar with local custom . . . The way I was brought up you always said "Amen" after you heard a prayer. You hear someone praying, after he finishes, you say "Amen" and drink a little wine.

'Cause that's what you just heard—a prayer. The way I

was brought up we called the particular prayer "the prayer for the dead." You just heard the prayer for the dead, and, fellow stuckholders, you didn't say "Amen" and you didn't even get to sip the wine.

What—You don't think this company is dead? Steel—you remember steel, don't you? Steel used to be an industry. Now heavy metal is a rock group.

This company is dead. Don't blame me. I didn't kill it. It was dead when I got here. It is too late for prayers, for even if the prayers were answered and a miracle occurred and the yen did this and the dollar did that and the infrastructure did the other thing, we would still be dead. Know why? Fiber-optics. New technologies. Obsolescence.

We're dead, all right. We're just not broke. And you know the surest way to go broke? Keep getting an increasing share of a shrinking market. Down the tubes. Slow but sure. You know, at one time there must have been dozens of companies making buggy whips. And I'll bet you anything the last one around was the one that made the best goddamned buggy whip you ever saw. How would you have liked to have been a stuckholder of that company?

You invested in a business. And that business is dead. Let's have the intelligence, let's have the decency, to sign the death certificate, collect the insurance and invest the money in something with a future.

Aha—But we can't, goes the prayer—we can't because we have a responsibility—a responsibility to our employees, our community ... What will happen to them? I got two words for that—"Who cares?" Care about them? They didn't care about you. They sucked you dry. You have no responsibility to them.

For the last ten years this company has bled your money. Did this Community care? Did they ever say, "I know things are tough. We'll lower your taxes, reduce water and sewer?" Check it out. We're paying twice what we paid ten years ago. And the mayor is making twice what he made ten years ago. And our devoted employees, after taking no increases for three years, are still making twice what they made ten years ago. And our stock is one-sixth what it was ten years ago.

Who cares? I'll tell you—me! I'm not your best friend—I'm your only friend. I care about you in the only way that matters in business. I don't make anything? I'm making you money. And, lest we forget, that's the only reason any of you became stuckholders in the first place. To make money. You don't care if they manufacture wire and cable, fry chicken, or grow tangerines. You want to make money. I'm making you money. I'm the only friend you got.

Take that money. Invest it somewhere else. Maybe—maybe you'll get lucky and it will be used productively—and if it is—you'll create more jobs and provide a service for the economy and—God forbid—even make a few bucks for yourself. Let the Government and the Mayor and the unions worry about what you paid them to worry about. And if anyone asks, tell them you gave at the plant.

And it pleases me that I'm called "Larry the Liquidator." You know why, fellow stuckholders? Because at my funeral you'll leave with a smile on your face . . . and a few bucks in your pocket. Now, that's a funeral worth having. (*Breathing heavily*, Garfinkle *pauses a beat and sits.*)

Bea: . . . Will the inspector of elections please collect the ballots.

The lights dim. Players are now in shadows. Coles *rises, moves slowly Center Stage.*

Coles: That's what happened. That's it. All of it.

Bea: Is there anyone entitled to vote who has not turned in a ballot?

Coles: It's happening everywhere. No one is immune.

Bea: To retain the present Board: 1,741,416.

Coles: I think the old man gave the speech of his life. I can't think how he could have said it better.

Bea: For the opposition slate: 2,219,901.

Coles: What do we do? Pass another law. There's already a law against murder. All he did was supply the weapon.

Bea: Not voting: 176,111.

Coles: Garfinkle won in a landslide. Didn't even need my votes. Cost me the second half million, but I feel good about that. I feel better about getting the first half million. I feel best it cost him money he didn't have to spend. That's the only kind of lasting satisfaction you get when you deal with people like him.

Bea: Mr. Garfinkle, your slate is elected.

Coles: He had the nerve to ask me to stay on while he dismembered the company. Even offered me a raise. I said "no," of course. There's a point at which we all draw the line.

Jorgenson: *(In his office.)* We can't leave now. I have to tell the men.

Bea: They know.

Jorgenson: . . . Already?

Bea: Let's go home. There'll be time tomorrow.

Jorgenson: Even . . . Ossie voted for him.

He exits. She remains.

Coles: He didn't take it well. From me . . . I think he expected it. Ossie . . . kind of threw him. With all his money you'd think he would have left. Gone somewhere nice . . . somewhere warm. He didn't. Stayed right here. Died almost two years later. Left more than thirty million.

Bea: Jorgy, you only made one mistake in your life. You lived two years too long.

Coles: Bea became executor of his estate. Bought the land the plant used to sit on. Put up a kind of . . . Employee Retraining Center—Actually placed a few people . . . about a hundred of the twelve hundred or so that worked there when the plant closed. It wasn't easy retraining middle-aged men who are used to working with their hands. Some went to work for McDonald's . . . or as night watchmen.

Me? I didn't do too badly. I moved back to Florida. Run a mid-sized division for a nationally known food processor. I won't ever run the company . . . but I'm financially secure. And you can't beat the weather.

Lights up on Garfinkle.

Garfinkle: I'm sorry, Kate. I'm surprised myself. See, you do bring out the best in me . . . Come—Ride back to New York with me . . . You worried it wouldn't look right? Don't. It's the perfect ending . . . Come.

She enters the playing area. Stops. Looks at him. He extends his arms to her, beckoning.

Come.

She doesn't move.

I got donuts in the car.

Coles: Kate and Garfinkle? Well, three months later, which is as soon as she could work things out at Morgan, Stanley, she went to work for him.

Kate *moves next to a seated* Garfinkle *in his office.*

She was very good. Three months after that she became his partner . . .

Her arm moves to the back of Garfinkle's *chair.*

. . . then his wife.

Her arm is around his shoulder. Garfinkle *beams.* Bea *exits.*

They have two kids. Set of twins. Call them their "little bull and little bear." Friend of mine saw them the other day . . . *(Moves to exit.)* Said he never saw them happier. *(Exits.)*

CURTAIN

The Longest Running Book on Broadway

And for the first time in paperback!

THE BURNS MANTLE THEATER YEARBOOK

THE BEST PLAYS OF 1988-89

Edited by Otis L. Guernsey Jr. and Jeffrey Sweet
Illustrated with drawings by AL HIRSCHFELD

The BURNS MANTLE "BEST PLAYS" YEARBOOK series is the source theater lovers have come to rely on for the most complete and thorough information on theater in America. Besides photographs of 1988-89 highlights, listings of all plays produced in New York and across the country, annual awards, and Hirschfeld drawings, this edition includes the complete text of *Emerald City*.

ARISTOCRATS	• Brian Friel
EASTERN STANDARD	• Richard Greenberg
ROAD	• Jim Cartright
THE HEIDI CHRONICLES	• Wendy Wasserstein
OTHER PEOPLE'S MONEY	• Jerry Sterner
LEND ME A TENOR	• Ken Ludwig
THE COCKTAIL HOUR	• A.R. Gurney
GUS AND AL	• Albert Innaurato
EMERALD CITY	• David Williamson
SHIRLEY VALENTINE	• Willy Russell

"The BEST PLAYS shelf has always been my favorite spot in any library. I used to get lost in its wonderful albums of photos, Hirschfelds, charts and good old fashioned Broadway yore for hours on end. Now that I've got my own BEST PLAYS shelf I get blissfully lost right here at home."

—Wendy Wasserstein

cloth • ISBN: 1-55783-057-6   paper • ISBN: 1-55783-056-8

APPLAUSE

SWEENEY TODD:
THE DEMON BARBER OF FLEET STREET

Music and Lyrics by Stephen Sondheim
Book by Hugh Wheeler

Here, with all its richness and power, is the monumental musical that revolves around the Fleet Street barber whose razor's swing takes many an unsuspecting victim and the woman who bakes them into pies. A major theatrical accomplishment, this thriller is as haunting to read as to watch on the stage.

The Applause Musical Library Edition includes Eugene Lee's set designs; Franne Lee's costume designs; production photographs; cast lists and credits; awards for all major productions; and the complete discography.

cloth • ISBN: 1-55783-065-7   paper • ISBN: 1-55783-066-5

A FUNNY THING HAPPENED ON THE
WAY TO THE FORUM

Music and Lyrics by Stephen Sondheim
Book by Burt Shevelove and Larry Gelbart

Here in the fresh guise of an original story are the classics of slapstick: conniving slaves, overamorous young lovers, lecherous old men, domineering wives, seductive courtesans and bragging soldiers. What happens when a wily slave, Pseudolus, contrives to obtain a fair virgin, Philia, for his master, Hero, in the free-wheeling Rome of 200 B.C. is the basis of these antic humors.

The Applause Musical Library Edition includes Tony Walton's set and costume designs; production photographs; cast lists and credits; awards for all major productions; and the complete discography.

cloth • ISBN: 1-55783-063-0   paper • ISBN: 1-55783-064-9

A LITTLE NIGHT MUSIC
Music and Lyrics by Stephen Sondheim
Book by Hugh Wheeler

A Little Night Music, suggested by Ingmar Bergman's film *Smiles of a Summer Night,* celebrates the ways of love on a turn-of-the-century Swedish estate and the Midsummer Eve follies of tangled liaisons and romantic intrigues.

The Applause Musical Library Edition includes Boris Aronson's set designs; Florence Klotz's costume designs; production photographs; cast lists and credits; awards for all major productions; lyrics deleted prior to the Broadway opening; and the complete discography.

cloth • ISBN: 1-55783-069-X   paper • ISBN: 1-55783-070-3

SUNDAY IN THE PARK WITH GEORGE
Music and Lyrics by Stephen Sondheim
Book by James Lapine

The young Georges Seurat was born in 1859 in Paris and died there in 1891. *"Dimanche, L'Après-Midi á l'Ile de la Grande Jatte"* ("A Sunday Afternoon on the Island of La Grande Jatte") was his second major work and *Sunday in the Park with George* is a work of fiction inspired by this masterpiece of Seurat and what little is known of his life.

The Applause Musical Library Edition includes Tony Straige's set designs; Patricia Zipprodt's and Ann Hould-Ward's costume designs; production photographs; cast lists and credits; awards for all major productions; and the complete discography.

cloth • ISBN: 1-55783-067-3   paper • ISBN: 1-55783-068-1

THE FANTASTICKS
Music by Harvey Schmidt
Words by Tom Jones
Introduction by Tom Jones
Illustrations by Harvey Schmidt

Thirtieth Anniversary Edition

The Fantasticks tells an age-old tale. Its ingredients are simple: a boy, a girl, two fathers, and a wall. Its scenery, a tattered cardboard moon, hovers over an empty wooden platform. With these bare essentials, Tom Jones and Harvey Schmidt launched a theatrical phenomenon unmatched the world over.

Clearly fantastic, this musical has set staggering records as the longest-running, most frequently produced musical ever. Now celebrating its thirtieth anniversary in New York, it has also enjoyed record runs worldwide. In 3,000 U.S. towns in 11,000 productions, and in over 700 productions in 68 other countries, *The Fantasticks* has enthralled audiences. Songs like "Soon It's Gonna Rain" and "Try to Remember" are recognized classics.

The Applause Musical Library Edition includes "Trying to Remember"—a fifty-page introduction about the origins and history of the show; new illustrations by Harvey Schmidt; production photographs (some in color) from around the world; cast lists and credits; the lyrics to a new song, "Abductions," written for the thirtieth anniversary by Jones and Schmidt; and a complete discography.

cloth • ISBN: 1-55783-074-6